W9-ADP-941

MODERN NOVELISTS

⌐HENRY JAMES⌐

Alan W. Bellringer

St. Martin's Press   New York

First published in the United States of America in 1988

Printed in China

ISBN 0–312–02056–2

Library of Congress Cataloging-in-Publication Data
Bellringer, Alan W.
Henry James
(Modern novelists)
Bibliography: p.
Includes index.
1. James, Henry, 1843–1916—Criticism and
interpretation. I. Title. II. Series.
PS2124.B44 1988   813′.4   88–4486
ISBN 0–312–02056–2

Contents

Acknowledgements

I am indebted to many friends and colleagues for help in understanding Henry James's writings. Among them I would single out Alun R. Jones for his stimulating exposition of James's idea of dramatised consciousness in seminars on literary criticism. I am thankful to my wife and family for forebearance and support during the period of composition of this book, and to Mrs Joyce Williams for secretarial assistance. I gratefully acknowledge contributions from the University College of North Wales towards research costs.

General Editor's Preface

The death of the novel has often been announced, and part of the secret of its obstinate vitality must be its capacity for growth, adaptation, self-renewal and even self-transformation: like some vigorous organism in a speeded-up Darwinian ecosystem, it adapts itself quickly to a changing world. War and revolution, economic crisis and social change, radically new ideologies such as Marxism and Freudianism, have made this century unprecedented in human history in the speed and extent of change, but the novel has shown an extraordinary capacity to find new forms and techniques and to accommodate new ideas and conceptions of human nature and human experience, and even to take up new positions on the nature of fiction itself.

In the generations immediately preceding and following 1914, the novel underwent a radical redefinition of its nature and possibilities. The present series of monographs is devoted to the novelists who created the modern novel and to those who, in their turn, either continued and extended, or reacted against and rejected, the traditions established during that period of intense exploration and experiment. It includes a number of those who lived and wrote in the nineteenth century but whose innovative contribution to the art of fiction makes it impossible to ignore them in any account of the origins of the modern novel; it also includes the so-called 'modernists' and those who in the mid- and late-twentieth century have emerged as outstanding practitioners of this genre. The scope is, inevitably, international; not only, in the migratory and exile-haunted world of our century, do writers refuse to heed national frontiers – 'English' literature lays claims to Conrad the Pole, Henry James the American, and Joyce the Irishman – but

geniuses such as Flaubert, Dostoevski and Kafka have had an
influence on the fiction of many nations.

Each volume in the series is intended to provide an
introduction to the fiction of the writer concerned, both for
those approaching him or her for the first time and for those
who are already familiar with some parts of the achievement in
question and now wish to place it in the context of the total
oeuvre. Although essential information relating to the writer's
life and times is given, usually in an opening chapter, the
approach is primarily critical and the emphasis is not upon
'background' or generalisations but upon close examination of
important texts. Where an author is notably prolific, major
texts have been selected for detailed attention but an attempt
has also been made to convey, more summarily, a sense of the
nature and quality of the author's work as a whole. Those who
want to read further will find suggestions in the select
bibliography included in each volume. Many novelists are, of
course, not only novelists but also poets, essayists, biographers,
dramatists, travel writers and so forth; many have practised
shorter forms of fiction; and many have written letters or kept
diaries that constitute a significant part of their literary output.
A brief study cannot hope to deal with all these in detail, but
where the shorter fiction and the non-fictional writings, public
and private, have an important relationship to the novels, some
space has been devoted to them.

For Mark

1

The Life of Henry James

Henry James's life, though not exceptionally long (he died at the age of seventy-two), covered such a world of change that it is odd to realise that he was a grown man in the mid-Victorian period. He kept so abreast of his times that as a senior writer he was able to strike the modern note before modernism arrived. Yet it is true that this twentieth-century novelist grew up way back in the era of romanticism. In 1843 when James was born, Balzac had just written his General Preface, Wordsworth became Poet Laureate, Chopin and Mendelssohn were still composing, and Turner found himself the hero of the first volume of *Modern Painters*, published anonymously by the unknown Ruskin. James, therefore, could think of Goethe and Scott as fairly recent predecessors.[1] If the earliness of early James is not self-evident, it is probably simply because it is not yet much known. Actually, when his first piece of fiction, 'A Tragedy of Error', was published in February 1864, Thackeray was just dead, Hawthorne still just alive, Dickens and George Eliot in full career and Hardy far from beginning. James's first novel, *Watch and Ward* (1871), precedes Hardy's *Desperate Remedies* and George Eliot's *Middlemarch*; his second, *Roderick Hudson* (1875), precedes her *Daniel Deronda* and Trollope's *The Prime Minister*. But James is somehow, imaginatively, not their contemporary. He eludes the nineteenth-century classification which strict chronology requires. He comes after the Victorians.

This advanced position of James in literary history is not merely a matter of his Americanness. Mark Twain, for instance, seems far more than the eight years James's senior that he was. It has to do with James's attitude to his work; he believed that the present and the immediate future were the best province of fiction, especially 'the future to which all our actual modern tendencies and leanings seem to build a sort of material

pathway'.[2] This statement, made in a letter to his twenty-two-
year-old sister, Alice, when he himself was twenty-six, is not
just a refusal to write historical novels, still less a word in
favour of science-fiction: it is a commitment to enlarge and
deepen experience *through* fiction rather than to reflect it *in*
fiction, a commitment to construct models for dialogue and
consciousness rather than to record talk and express the self.
James is not, then, so much the child of his age as the father of
the next. Bred in modern cities, beneficiary of an educational
free hand, inveterate traveller from infancy, Henry James had
all the advantage of being an old head on young shoulders.
Culturally precocious, with a foot in two continents, he became
in turn an Arnoldian before his time, an agnostic before Huxley
coined the word, a proto-aesthete and a pre-modernist modern.
On discovering his brother William James's philosophy of
pragmatism, he told him that he himself had 'unconsciously
pragmatised' all his life.[3] Habitually anticipating everything
and devoutly ambitious for literary success, the young James
naturally collected interviews with the famous as others collect
rocks or postcards. He was acknowledged by Emerson on his birth
as a 'new friend' and by Thackeray a short time later as 'Buttons'.[4]
After this auspicious start he met everybody he could in the
intellectual world, from Darwin and Dickens to Turgenev and
Flaubert, on their own, or his own, ground. No one ever worked
more comprehensively than did Henry James at being a writer.
He had the American super-professional attitude to it. When he
became a novelist, he seemed a new phenomenon, a school to
himself, subtly critical of other novelists, fastidious about
technique, so finely intelligent that he must be in a different
class from the rest. To read his *Portrait of a Lady* straight after
reading, say, George Eliot's *Daniel Deronda* is to take the
measure of this enhanced selectivity, tact and self-effacement. It
is a fact that James, who was willing eventually to be known as
the Master, made literature his life far more than ever he
turned his life into literature. This sense which he had, a sense
of the priority of literature, and above all of the novel ('It is art
that *makes* life', he told the bewildered H. G. Wells),[5] always
makes it very difficult to place James in any tradition or milieu.
He is one for whom a context, whether it is national, historical
or philosophical, is not lying to hand, I think, but has to be
supplied as he goes.

The first major influence on James was his father, Henry James senior, who certainly had unusual ideas. A non-church-going Christian of harmless but vigorously promulgated views, the elder James converted his wife entirely to his own way of thinking, but had less success with his five children. Himself one of thirteen children, he had inherited (after litigation) a comfortable income from his own father, a Presbyterian Irish immigrant, who had prospered in New York city and state in land, banking and salt and left over three million dollars on his death in 1832. Educated at Albany Academy, Schenectady Union College and Princeton Theological Seminary, James's father reacted against this stern Protestant upbringing by adopting a vague, unorthodox theism of his own, independent of any discipline or party. He believed he had penetrated the mystery of Swedenborg, the eighteenth-century Swedish theologian, and could marry it to the socialism of Fourier, who had argued for the reorganisation of early nineteenth-century French society into phalanges or small communes. So armed, or disarmed, Henry James senior published a whole series of books with titles like *Moralism and Christianity* (1850) or *Society, the Redeemed Form of Man* (1879), which were little regarded, even in America. The contents, however, were known to his son, through the medium of conversational advice. The elder James saw God as a saving agent at work within the passions of universal man; and America, the New World, was the home of this universal man, freed from the individual peculiarities which so absorbed the interest of a European novelist like Dickens. So America might, virtually at any moment, be transfigured into a redeemed society, harmonious beyond the most visionary of expectations. The main obstacle to the realisation of this version of the American dream lay, according to James's father, in the national tendency to moralism, or self-righteousness; in the narrow, Puritanical, legalistic conformity to rules and prohibitions, which was against the whole spirit of his social ideal. Much of this attack on moralism, mildly satiric as it was, and perhaps the benign faith in civilised harmony, though in an implied form only, rubbed off on the son. But Henry James senior's genial principles found their most practical outlet in the liberal and peripatetic education of his children.

Henry James was born on 15 April 1843 at 21 Washington Place in New York. From 1845 to 1847 James's family lived in

Albany, a hundred miles north of New York, near his
grandmother's. From 1847 to 1855 they settled near Union
Square, New York, where the young James read *Punch* and
heard *David Copperfield* read out; he saw plays by Shakespeare
and Boucicault,[6] and was taught by many teachers without
being permanently attached to any teaching establishment. His
father was so opposed to pedantry and dogma that, as James
later wrote, the 'literal played in our education as small a part
as it perhaps ever played in any', but the 'presence of paradox
was so bright among us'.[7] Henry was the second of the children.
The two younger boys had little of the family literary ability,
but Alice, the youngest, the future diarist, proved a lively if
nervous companion, and William, the eldest, the future professor
of philosophy, born sixteen months before Henry, was so gifted
that the latter to some extent always lived in his shadow. Even
after William's death in 1910, Henry James began the first
volume of his autobiography, *A Small Boy and Others* (1913), in
apparent doubt as to which of the two the small boy is. The
'primary figure' whose early life he is presenting is William
James; yet the world which composes itself around this figure
soon becomes 'the world within', that is memories of Henry
James's own youthful consciousness. With typical indirectness
James approaches himself, admitting he can scarcely convey
'how prevailingly and almost exclusively, during years and
years, the field was animated and the adventure conditioned for
me by my brother's nearness and that play of genius in him of
which I had never had a doubt from the first'.[8] Sadly, this
fraternal assurance of genius was not reciprocated. William
James was to dislike in his brother's initial work 'something
cold, thin-blooded and priggish suddenly popping in and
freezing the genial current' and eventually damned the later
novels for mustiness of plot, fencing in of the dialogue,
evasiveness of style and lack of vigour in the action. 'Your
methods and my ideals seem the reverse, the one of the other',[9]
was the final snub. Henry James was baffled but not checked
by this frankness. Though the role of humble younger brother
which he kept up brought painful episodes, he continued to
give to all members of his family his first loyalty. James had
been doomed to follow in his brother's footsteps, never to
overtake him, on various courses at home and abroad, in
science, languages and art, culminating temporarily in the

Harvard Law School; repeatedly he had to resign himself to falling short of the standards of William.

In view of the diffidence which this relationship induced and the irregularity of his curriculum, it is remarkable how learned James became. He was most impressive in French, in which he conversed and corresponded at ease with experts no less than Daudet and even Flaubert himself, but he was also 'very much at home in Italian', sharing his learning eagerly 'by the adroitest of hints'; as we are told.[10] He knew, evidently from early on, all the classics of English, American and French literature as well as the best-known German texts in German and the Russian ones in translation. He knew a great deal about art, not only from Ruskin, but at first hand, though his taste remained, if not heavy, then rather conservative. Music appealed to him much less, even boring him. It was artists and actors whose acquaintance he sought rather than that of composers and singers. Henry James was no systematic scholar or philosophical intellectual with a scientific curiosity like George Eliot's or his brother William's. His uncomfortableness in German circles – the fact that, contrary to William's suggestion, he baulked at becoming the 'unworthiest adoptive grandchild of the fatherland'[11] – marked him off from them most significantly and ironically enabled him to escape seeming dated by Germanophilia, which was the fate of so many other older writers (not Conrad, incidentally, either) when the Anglo-German conflict arose and deepened towards the end of his career. It does indicate, however, a certain limitation to Henry James's seriousness. Generally as a literary figure James strikes us as a shade or two more limited than, say, Matthew Arnold, whom he so revered, or T. S. Eliot, who so liked him. James's critical views on poetry followed the conventional late-Romantic tastes of his day. It was only on the novel, ultimately, that James was an original thinker. But this specialism is really an aspect of his American acuteness. He chose the novel when it was still the dominant literary form. He devoted all his reading to that. He practised and expounded its art all his working life.

Yet he was not trained to do so; James was not brought up to write novels, as, say, Jane Austen was. He did it entirely off his own bat. His father, horrified by anything approaching priggishness, preferred him to cultivate his general humane leanings rather than to prepare himself for a career.

Vocationalism was too narrow, even if the vocation were for
writing novels. Henry James senior had little interest in his
children's 'mastery of *any* art or craft', said his son, since he
declined 'to dabble in the harshness of practical precautions or
impositions'.[12] Rather, his awareness that his second son was
such a 'devourer of libraries, and an immense writer of novels
and dramas'[13] made him anxious and determined him to send
his son to a technical school for a time. His father was concerned
lest he 'read too many novels, or at least read them too
attentively',[14] remarks James, a little unfairly. That was in
Geneva in 1859, and the seventeen-year-old James archly
confessed within the next few months to having attempted some
literary work in private; 'to no style am I a stranger, there is
none which has not been adorned by the magic of my touch'.[15]
Indeed the letters from this period describing Europe to an
American friend show a lively style of observation.

The cumulative impressions of foreign travel were probably
as powerful a stimulus to James's first literary efforts as were
the contents of libraries. James had had a long apprenticeship
to touring; at the age of six months he was taken to live near
Windsor Castle in England and from there in the following year
to Paris. For a formative period from 1855 to 1858 he was
abroad with the family, living in Geneva, London, Paris and
Boulogne. His early impressions of European scenes and
characters he never forgot. After a year in Newport, Rhode
Island, he returned to Europe with his family in 1859 and 1860,
staying at Geneva and Bonn. From 1860 to 1864, they were
again staying at Newport. It was the period of the American
Civil War, but James, owing to a back injury sustained while
he was helping to fight a fire, took no part in the conflict. By
the time he was twenty-one, approximately one-third of James's
life had been spent in foreign countries and virtually the whole
of it in reading and in learning languages, including Latin. He
was thus in many ways an untypical American; a privileged,
cultured, cosmopolitan Easterner, accustomed to comparing life
in different countries from a standpoint that was frequently
shifting relative to the objects perceived. With such an oscillating
experience of 'home', it is not surprising that the uncertainty
factor should loom so large in James's fiction without panic. He
exploited and enjoyed his comparative freedom. Writing in old
age of the American milieu, James remarked that he had not

outlived the satisfaction of 'being in New England without being of it'.[16] He valued not only the detachment and mobility which the inherited financial independence conferred on him, but also his origin in a tolerant climate. James was careful not to give the reader of his autobiography the impression that his father was '*too* irresponsible' in chopping and changing his education or too impulsive in their 'journeyings to and fro', for he regarded the lack of continuity as essentially generous.[17]

Newport played an important part in James's development, not only in providing him with scenes for some of the most memorable episodes in his stories, but also because of its artistic fraternity. It was a young Newport artist, John La Farge, whose friendly encouragement gave a definite direction to James's literary ambitions in the 1860s. La Farge had had personal contact with French writers like Saint-Beuve, Flaubert and the Goncourts while he was in Paris; he now introduced James to the novels of Balzac and the tales of Prosper Merimée, suggesting also that he read Browning. James's first works submitted for publication (and rejected) included a translation of a Merimée story and a review of a translation of a German play which he had seen acted in Boston, called *Fanchon the Critic*, itself derived from a novel by George Sand. Play-going and reviewing suited James more than law studies at Harvard (he lost a case he was defending in a moot court), and when he left college prematurely he took back to Newport with him certain manuscripts that were not law-notes but were 'small sickly seed, no doubt,' of fiction.[18] The seed took, for when he offered a short-story, 'A Tragedy of Error', to the short-lived *Continental Monthly* of New York, it was accepted and published anonymously in February 1864. Set in what is probably Le Havre, 'A Tragedy of Error' has some melodramatic and some distancing elements. There is a conspiratorial Frenchwoman in it, a cool, gentlemanly lover and two observant servants. The lady hires a boatman, whom she has just met, to drown her lame husband on his return from America: the boatman by mistake drowns the lover instead of the husband, who is glimpsed limping homewards at the conclusion. The tale is remarkable for its authentic French atmosphere, its air of having been translated from the French, but it is more than an exercise in the French manner. It demonstrates an intelligence of technique which can handle economy, indirectness and selection without irrelevance. It was a most unsentimental beginning.

Immediately after his first appearance in print, James moved with the family up to Boston, the centre of New England culture. Here his literary contacts multiplied. James T. Fields, editor of the *Atlantic Monthly*, invited him to literary salons, where he met Longfellow, J. R. Lowell, Mrs H. B. Stowe and others. James was now well-placed to take advantage of the increased activity then occurring in the world of literary periodicals. Lowell and C. E. Norton, the new editors of the *North American Review*, welcomed book reviews from James. There were other opportunities. In 1865 E. L. Godkin, with the support of Henry James senior, started the monthly *Nation*, for the first volume of which James wrote nine reviews. The most influential admirer of his stories, W. D. Howells, joined the *Nation*'s editorial staff in 1866. In the same year the *Galaxy* was launched in New York. It was in these journals that James's first signed short stories appeared, some of them in instalments. From 1866 onwards James was living with his parents at 20 Quincy Street, Cambridge (facing Harvard yard), their last home. It was here that he wrote his series of long tales, some with the American Civil War as a background, some introducing the supernatural, almost all concerned with disappointment and sadness in personal relations. Generally, however, this violence and loss are reflected in peaceful surroundings. In 'The Story of a Year' (*Atlantic Monthly*, March 1865), for example, when Jack Ford goes off to the war to be fatally wounded, the narrator explains why the story remains at home. 'My own taste has always been for unwritten history, and my present business is with the reverse of the picture.' The allegiance here is to the tradition of domestic epic going back through George Eliot to Goethe's *Hermann und Dorothea*, and yet neither of them would have turned the picture round to its reverse. James's image is daringly analytic and disturbing. The tale itself, though ambiguous, takes itself a little too seriously to live up to the disturbing expectations aroused by the narrator. All the early tales are interesting: regarding love coolly, avoiding action where they can, dwelling on anticipations and aftermaths, sometimes leaving the reader to fill in and finish off. There are experiments in autobiographical narration and historical decor, but nothing expansive as yet, nothing of potential scope.

As the 1860s wore on, with James's elder brother and one or two of his friends on extended sojourns in Europe, he began to question his position as an American writer. Was he to be another Bostonian, or something more, a man of the future? James believed that the heroic age of New England innocence, with its struggle against slavery and its effort to transcend evil by setting up more natural modes of living, was past. The need now was to look back from the frontier towards Europe, to acquire a more self-critical civilisation through international contacts and cross-fertilisation in the humane arts. 'I think that to be an American is an excellent preparation for culture',[19] James wrote in 1867, enabling one, he meant, to pick and assimilate forms of civilisation and to contribute the American moral consciousness to the work of the new age: the literature of the future would be produced by the fused national tendencies of the world. In this avant-garde mood James determined to revisit Europe on his own, financed, of course, by the family, so as to observe again those national tendencies with the eyes of a man of twenty-six. He reached Liverpool in February 1869, but hardly observed *it*. In London a more exciting type of observation awaited him – interviewing celebrities, whom he could describe in letters home. C. E. Norton was there, making many of the introductions. James met Darwin, George Eliot, G. H. Lewes, Frederic Harrison, Ruskin, Rossetti, Morris and others, a sensational visiting-list. He toured in the Malvern area and then stayed in an Oxford college. In May 1867 he left for the Continent, but here contacts were fewer and more modest, and James concentrated on scenery and architecture. His long letters home give his impressions of Venice, Florence, Rome, Genoa, then Paris, and Malvern again. His family, though appreciative, may have wondered whether he was not wasting his time. He was ignoring German philosophy, certainly, but he was becoming aware of workable themes for his fiction. The visit gave rise to several new tales with European settings, notably 'A Passionate Pilgrim' (*Atlantic Monthly*, March–April 1871), the story which gave its title to James's first book, a collection of six stories, not published until 1875. James's ascription of prominence to this piece is well-judged. 'A Passionate Pilgrim' is, in fact, the first characteristically Jamesian piece of fiction. In it we find evocative travel-writing firming up a plot of frustration and anger, in which a sick

American is thwarted of both marriage and an inheritance in England through the opposition of a Tory villain. Familiar Jamesian figures come together for the first time: the sympathetic but unengaged narrator, the renunciatory young woman of a certain age, the professional man with his 'easy morality', and the solemn butler. But what gives 'A Passionate Pilgrim' its strength beneath the expression of a romantic American longing to reenter his English heritage is a counterveiling pride in America's own values. We note with embarrassment the narrator's persistent efforts to invest England with literary charm. There is a Dickensian coffee-room in London and, less plausibly, a town-centre (Worcester's) 'where surely Miss Austen's heroines, in chariots and curricles, must often have come a shopping for swan's-down boas and high lace mittens'. Fortunately this off-key literary archaeology falters ironically when the story reaches Oxford. Suddenly, amid routine admiration for this 'dim and sacred ideal of the Western intellect', the main interest focuses on one Rawson. He is a shabby cicerone, late of Wadham College, obviously an unsuccessful product of the English system. Rawson, being 'the victim of some fatal depreciation in the market value of pure gentility', is inevitably bitter about the English and envious of the Americans. In the end Rawson gets his passage to the States paid for him by the hero, so that he can get out of this 'awful England'. This return of the tale upon itself suggests a divided Jamesian commitment to the two worlds of Europe and American and their ways.

The effective structuring of 'A Passionate Pilgrim' reveals the influence of Matthew Arnold's ideas on Henry James. The balanced comparison of cultures is an Arnoldian prescription. James had been trying since 1865 to live up to Arnold's ideal of the disinterested critic and detached observer of life. He often reproduced Arnold's satiric serenity of tone in the prose of his own narrators, as well as in his personal approach to people and life. James's concept of his role as a writer was informed by Arnold's image of the spectator who penetrates the world's secrets by renouncing his own pleasure. To see things as in themselves they really are, the novelist must not become too involved with them. Particularly has he to avoid the participation that is marriage.

James's disinclination to marry naturally invites speculation as to its cause. Was James a latent homosexual? Nothing in James's effusive friendships with men, which multiplied as he grew older, is incompatible with the attribution of a homoerotic tendency to him, except perhaps their complete shamelessness, which would be unlikely at that period if he meant sex. James was not undersexed, but he was too imaginatively curious about both sexes to be vulnerably bisexual himself, too devoted to words to let love put him off, and too keen to assimilate everyone else's experience to risk letting his writing suffer from absorption in his own personal relationships. The unexpected death of his cousin Minny Temple in 1870 shocked him deeply and seemed to close the door on the possibility of love; not that James had done much more than admire her intellectual grace, enjoy her company and respond to her untravelled American open-mindedness. He felt that Minny's death marked the close of his youth, but he kept certain of her qualities in mind when constructing his favourite female characters. This loss no doubt confirmed him in his adoption of Arnold's spectator-persona. James began to argue that a certain type of bachelor could play a useful, beneficent and civilising part in society. 'He keeps up the tone of humanity'; he may even 'forward the cause of civilization'.[20] He projected the idea in several of his characters. Mixed opportunities, partings, failures, renunciations, sacrifices, even absences, play an important, hardly negative, role in James's fiction; it is his achievers who often seem so obstructive. Non-alignment is frequently for James the condition of enhanced understanding rather than of mere missing out. James worked on non-dialectical principles. His novels as a whole achieve as disinterested and balanced a presentation of multiple conflicting tensions as Arnold could have wished. James feared that embroilment in experience itself would have impaired his power to produce his texts.

With a timely avoidance of the Franco-Prussian War, James returned to Boston in 1870, looking now to America to provide him with the subject of his first novel. He would have liked it to be a great novel. But he saw America increasingly as a cultural backwater, comparatively boring and arid. In this mood he predictably came up with a thin theme for the novel, which he could stretch to only eleven chapters. *Watch and Ward* was serialised in the *Atlantic Monthly* from August to December 1871. The plot is a version of the Pygmalion myth. A bachelor who

has just been jilted adopts a twelve-year-old orphan girl, met
by chance, and succeeds in a long-term plan to marry her
without entailing her resentment. These events could be set
anywhere, and James coyly avoids mentioning Boston till
halfway through. Characteristically, it is a visit to Europe,
mentioned but not described, which effects the transformation
of the ward: it enables the girl's nature to rise calmly to
maturity, 'fed by the sources of aesthetic delight' (Chapter
VII). The contextual vacuum is matched by a hiatus in the
psychology. Love is left scrupulously out of the account. The
heroine is beset by unworthy suitors, and the hero, not having a
'lover's love' for her, wins her by exercising his basic good
nature. She discovers his secret of the universe: it consists in the
fact that her guardian was 'the only man in it who had a heart'
(Chapter XI). With the cards so stacked for him, it was, we
may say, a push-over. *Watch and Ward* is not without irony, but
it did not please James. He did not revise it for publication in
book-form till 1878. It is below the standard of the best short
fiction, which James was writing at the time, such as 'Travelling
Companions' (*Atlantic Monthly*, November–December 1870),
being, unlike that, somewhat forced. In 1872, in search of more
promising material, he persuaded his father to finance a new
trip to Europe, the cost of which he hoped to defray by
contributing travel-pieces to the *Nation*.

On this tour James was at first accompanied by his sister and
aunt, but when they returned in the autumn of 1872 he stayed
on, remaining, in fact, till 1874. He lived for a time in Paris,
mixing mainly with fellow-Americans, and then spent much of
1873 in Italy, again mainly among American artists and friends,
with the summer in Switzerland and Germany. It was at this
period that James's principal subject took shape in his mind –
what could be termed degrees of expatriation. As a regular
American visitor to American expatriates, he knew he could
make something of Americans resident abroad. The European
scene provided him with a historically and visually fascinating
backcloth for his studies of semi-permanent American exiles.
This subject derives an added piquancy from the fact that the
divided loyalties of such people make love a difficult experience
for them to sustain. So James had to hand a particularly
appropriate context for those staples of fiction, the impossible
romance and the unhappy marriage. Inserted into this pattern

could go examples of national types, varieties of artists, journalists and men of affairs. But the whole would be controlled from the viewpoint of an observer-figure not unlike James himself.

The major result of these designs was *Roderick Hudson*, which James began in Florence in 1874 and completed in America in 1875. The eponymous hero is a young American sculptor of a romantic temperament whose experience of Europe (mostly Rome) leads to failure and extinction. The plot has a typically Jamesian structure: with a preliminary episode set in New England, a long central sequence among the cultural riches of Europe, a dénouement when the Americans left behind come after their relative, and final scenes of tension and dismay set in the Alps. The overall effect is tragi-comic, owing to the assumption that art is superior to love. The novel presents various views of art; it weighs the New England mistrust of artistic sensuality against the European manipulation of talent for non-artistic ends. The whole debate is conducted with entertaining satire. Less happy are the actual works of art described, which are conventionally romantic, but convey an unintended excitement over the male nude. This element occupies not only Roderick Hudson, the 'nervous nineteenth-century Apollo' (Chapter XV), but also his innocent mentor and patron, Rowland Mallet, who sponsors his trip and chaperones him for a good part of it. Mallet, a figure of incorruptible modesty but no practical, political or artistic talents, is made, surprisingly, to fall in love with Mary Garland, Hudson's fiancée from West Nazareth, though James cannot quite bring himself to assert that he wins her in the end. The rivalry between the demure but intelligent Mary and the much more worldly, beautiful and inconsistent Christina Light, the adventuress with a soft spot, shows James exploiting, not for the last time, a traditional fictional contrast between two female types. There are several loose ends in *Roderick Hudson*, but the mixed aesthetic and moral curiosity of Rowland Mallet is handled with considerable delicacy. The novel deserved its favourable reception because of its width of interest and astuteness of observation. Two of the men James most respected in the world, Turgenev and Matthew Arnold, said they liked it. Arnold, in his first long piece on the civilisation of the United States, 'A Word about America' (*Nineteenth Century*, May 1882), called *Roderick Hudson* 'one of the best' of James's works, drawing attention to the character of Striker in it as representatively Philistine.[21] Also R. H. Hutton thought *Roderick Hudson* 'skilful and subtle', referring to Henry James's 'great talents' (*Spectator*, July 1879), yet he also felt its total effect was dreary and pessimistic. It was the revised, first English edition of 1879 that was having this impact. James's success should not be exaggerated. *Roderick Hudson* had sold only about three thousand copies by the early 1880s, far fewer than works by W. D. Howells and Mark Twain. Yet, even if the public did not take easily to a sophisticated American novelist who eschewed action, moral uplift and religious debate, James's reputation was advancing.[22]

In November 1875 James settled in Europe for good; at first in Paris, where he was the correspondent of the *New York Tribune*. Apart from reporting on current drama and art, he was most interested in cultivating the friendship of celebrated French novelists, such as Flaubert, Daudet, Zola and Maupassant, some of whose behaviour repelled him, however. His mixed feelings for French ways leave their mark on *The American*, which was being serialised at this time. Late in 1876 James left France for Britain, which became his adopted country for the remainder of his life – for forty years. The pattern of living which he now established for himself consisted of three practices; keeping rented rooms in London, visiting friends (often in country-houses) in various parts of Britain, and spending extended summers on the Continent, usually in Italy. It was a solo existence, supported by servants, dependent on loyal friends; at first on the edge, later in the centre and finally at the top of society. Much time was devoted to his correspondence, which is too vast to have been published yet in full, but which was largely personal rather than intellectual in content. James also used London clubs, at first the Athenaeum, and then the Liberal-minded Reform. He followed the events of the English season, watched the boat race, dined with writers, artists and politicians, attended the theatre, talked and walked. Now he began increasingly to place his shorter fiction and essays in British periodicals and published his novels on both sides of the Atlantic. It was the time of the best-known works of his early maturity, *The Europeans* (1878), *Washington Square* (1880) and *The Portrait of a Lady* (1880–1). His study *Hawthorne*

(1879) contained a vivid account of the defects of American culture, which provoked sharp reactions from across the Atlantic. James welcomed the controversy as likely to make him a familiar name; it was 'a great piece of good fortune to have stirred up such a clatter', though it only confirmed his view that England was the higher civilisation of the two, 'in literary respects'.[23] There was a sexual dimension to the furore in so far as it appertained to 'Daisy Miller' (1878) and 'An International Episode' (1878–9), where the boldness of American women is at issue. James's critical-comic stance towards these nice international misunderstandings afforded him a fashionable prominence at parties, theatre-boxes and political weekends. There was even a vogue for 'Daisy Miller' hats. James was not averse to social success. He once told E. S. Nadal, the second secretary at the American Legation in London, 'I think a position in society is a legitimate object of ambition.'[24] In a sense he had always had a position; he was merely absorbed in shifting and securing it. He felt absolutely at home living in London. 'Such an experience is an education – it fortifies the character and embellishes the mind . . . and for one who takes it as I take it, London is on the whole the most possible form of life. I take it as an artist and as a bachelor; as one who has the passion of observation and whose business is the study of human life.'[25] James actually wrote this appreciation of London life while he was back in Boston after five years' absence. He spent much of the period from 1881 to 1883 in the States, attending his parents' funerals, meeting William James's wife and their son, dramatising two of his stories and arranging with his publishers for a fourteen-volume cheap edition of most of the fiction which he had written up to that date.

He returned to his lodgings in Piccadilly in September 1883, not to revisit America for twenty-one years. James was now in his forties and about to enter a period of uncertainty and disappointment. At the start of this phase of doubt, which lasted on and off for about twelve years, James wrote one rather specialised masterpiece, *The Bostonians* (1885–6), followed by two sprawling narratives focussed on contemporary political and aesthetic problems, *The Princess Casamassima* (1885–6) and *The Tragic Muse* (1889–90). The first of these massive novels is mainly satiric, exposing American gullibility at the hands of publicists for 'causes' (it proved unpopular in America, from which already James began to feel cut off); the second attempts a realistic investigation of anarchist and trade union groups in Britain with uneven results, especially in the dialogue; and the third, a promisingly attractive 'society' novel, featuring diplomats, actresses and artists, almost falls apart owing to its ambling pace, over-spacious double plot and uncharacteristic ponderousness of tone. Though deeply rewarding in many respects, none of these works served in the public's view to crown James's previous achievements. James's career was sagging under the weight of a naturalism to which he was not suited and which no longer suited the times. What was happening was that the first uncertainty as to the direction the novel itself could take was coming through. The age of democracy had begun in Britain, the growth of mass culture was visible, the pace of life was quickening, and the three-decker novel, especially if pervaded by a refined, tentative awareness like James's, hardly fitted the bill. Britain's position of world-leadership was under threat, a subject which fascinated James. He had 'a general sense of rocks ahead in the foreign relations' of Britain and was both touched and thrilled by what he detected, namely the beginning of the decline of Old England, whose 'great precarious, artificial empire' would eventually have to be given up.[26] James made some remarkably prescient analyses of the trends of British history, but the appropriate aspects of these developments, as far as fiction is concerned, were the lower classes and the British abroad, neither of which James was well qualified to handle. James himself would have to give up the precarious empire of fictional realism. His novels would have to do more than chronicle the age.

In 1885 James moved from Piccadilly across to Kensington, to a flat in the new, smart De Vere Mansions, where he was to live till 1898. Here he went in for new intimate friendships: with young literary Americans settling in Europe and acting to some extent as his disciples; with British writers like R. L. Stevenson, Mrs Humphry Ward, Vernon Lee and Edmund Gosse; with theatrical and artistic personalities of both London and New York. He was ceasing to emphasise the contrasts between American and English life and reverting to his original forecast of a coming together of cultures, at least in the form of a coming together of these two branches of the one culture. In 1888 he wrote to William James about this 'big Anglo-Saxon total, destined to such an amount of melting together', as he thought, that the life of the two countries could now even be treated as continuous or convertible.[27] James was beginning to anticipate the global village. He saw himself more and more as the explorer of the refined conscience and intelligent imagination in a demotic, commercialised, sporadically violent, media-orientated society where traditional values – resistant still, perhaps, in classically-based national cultures like the Italian and the French – were giving way under challenge. However, modern tensions and troubles were becoming universal, he feared. And so, such topics as divorce, psychological illness, adolescent awareness, the conscience of the artist, the guilt of the rich, the invasion of privacy, paranormal experience and nervous obsession offered themselves to the fascinated James as themes for new problem novels – fiction for a world given over relentlessly to political stridency, to militarism, to strikes, to professional sport, to organised gambling, to technological innovation and to *Kitsch* for the semi-literate masses. These visions cut right across international boundaries, so that James's existing role as a wanderer between two worlds became a distinct advantage. James reacted to this crisis of change at the end of the nineteenth century, not, as other novelists like Hardy or Shaw did, by abandoning fiction altogether for other forms, but by altering fiction itself in an experimental or modernist direction.

James did make for a time, it is true, a serious attempt to strike out as a playwright, partly by adapting previous stories for the stage and partly by devising plays which could be converted quickly back into novels. But James was far too inward a writer to master fully the techniques of drama. The venture foundered in 1895 with the shocking reception awarded to *Guy Domville*. This piece, specially written by James as a play, concerns, of all the unlikely things, an eighteenth-century English aristocrat who, though trained to be a Roman Catholic priest, proposes marriage to his tutor's mother. Finally disillusioned, Guy resolves to enter a monastery. James had clearly gone off the rails. Though the play's antiquated dialogue is sometimes quaintly effective, H. G. Wells was undoubtedly right to comment, 'the entire workmanship was too delicate for acting', a diagnosis which pointed to 'an early deathbed' for James's play.[28] What appalled James was that a section of the

audience at the St James's Theatre hissed him when he came
on to take his author's bow. Fortunately, James had never
given up writing prose-fiction during his five years' wrestling
with Thespis: some of his best sort stories belong to these years,
notably 'The Pupil' (1891), 'The Real Thing' (1892) and 'Owen
Wingrave' (1892), though this last also went into a play version
which, in two letters, James brilliantly defended against Shaw's
accusation of moral inexplicitness.[29] He now determined to
make use of what he had learnt as a dramatist in strengthening
the structure of his novels. He confided to his notebooks
scenarios or plans for his stories, at first mainly about English
society at the upper end, with alternating scenes of conflict and
passages of descriptive thoughts. This new concentration on
economy, form and technique marks the recovery of purpose in
James's career and inaugurates his spell as the most formidable
writer of his day with the most demanding output.

The tally of late James works begins with *The Spoils of Poynton*
(1896) and reaches ten novels and three dozen tales; it is
extremely impressive by any standards in quality and quantity.
The late style is always difficult and gets too odd and sluggish
towards the end. But it repays care and rereading, and for
many becomes addictive. James's main ploy is to slip back and
forward between elaborate notation of inner consciousness
(using fantastic figures of speech and syntactical inversions)
and cryptic dialogue. Colloquial allusions and teasing lacunae
give the reader plenty to do. At the same time James becomes
more of a legerdemainist with his plot, with much of preview
and retrospect in place of the real thing, while the manipulation
of point of view throws fundamental doubt on the nature of the
action and on the evaluation of its consequences. Sensing the
breakdown of Victorian certainties in the perception of science,
psychology, moral philosophy and art, James exploits the function
of the unreliable narrator to produce dense fictional texts of
intriguing ambiguity and fertile interpretative potential. The
sheer scale and uniqueness of these works brought James the
prestige which was his due. He became in his last years the
central literary personality of the age, holding a position similar
to that of Dr Samuel Johnson in the later eighteenth century.

France, Italy and English country-seats were still on James's
itinerary, to be plied for scenes for his stories. He also developed
a liking for English seaside resorts, especially Bournemouth and

Torquay. In 1896 the summer brought him to a friend's cottage near Rye in East Sussex. He found that district endearing for its historical picturesqueness and rural quiet. The peace and prettiness of the whole land there, he wrote, had been good to him, 'and I stay on with unabated relish',[30] moving for a time into the vicarage in the town itself. In 1897, when Lamb House in Rye fell vacant, James obtained the lease; in 1898 he moved in; in 1899 he bought it freehold. James was now a small-town householder, still with the Reform Club as a London winter base. Rye was not exactly a retreat, since several outstanding novelists lived within range, notably Crane, Wells, Kipling and Conrad; and other writers paid him visits, including Edith Wharton, Gissing, Ford Madox Hueffer (later Ford), Chesterton and Hugh Walpole. James employed a typist and a gardener, who lived close by; the domestic servants, including a house-boy, later James's valet, lived in. Life was tranquil, geared to the manufacture of typescript. James's reliance on stenography dates from 1897 when a pain in his right wrist induced him to buy a typewriter. He began dictating straight to the stenographer at the machine during *What Maisie Knew* (exactly at what point is disputed); it affected his prose style with a kind of oral cast, which includes an excess of parentheses and circumlocutions, but no blurring. James was not inhospitable to new machinery, either in his home or in his prose: he accepted electric light and the telephone, used telegrams, tried out the cinema, took up cycling, went motoring and even used an aeroplane once (as a comparison).[31] But applied science was never an enthusiasm in itself to James, merely a slight amenity to the cultivation of humane feelings. Life at Lamb House was dominated by those feelings (with a prejudice in favour of dogs and against cats). Friends and relatives were entertained on a rather lavish American scale. Younger members of the James family came over to sample the hospitality or be taken out in London and Paris. During the summer of 1900 at Lamb House James began writing the first of the three long novels which were to crown his success. The pattern of older and younger American adults who are in Europe for one reason or another is common to *The Ambassadors* (1903), *The Wings of the Dove* (1902, but written second) and *The Golden Bowl* (1904). In these works James integrated his old international theme with his new methods; multiple or limited perspective, interplay of impressionistic consciousness and witty dialogue, and subtle selection of incident.

Certainly *The Ambassadors*, which James considered the 'most proportioned' and rounded[32] of his productions, displays a great advance on, say, *Roderick Hudson*. The New England episode at the beginning of the earlier novel is there in the later one only in reminiscence and conversation, as Strether, a figure much resembling Mallet in temper and inclinations, reconsiders the point of his life during a stay in Chester, London and Paris. In place of the aspiring genius of Roderick Hudson with his unconvincing sculptures, James brings forward the uncertain character of Chad Newsome, who could only toy with artistic training and eventually, to Strether's surprise, but not the reader's, precipitates himself into advertising and returns to the family firm in Massachusetts, as requested by his mother. Instead of the glamorous Princess Christina of *Roderick Hudson* and *The Princess Casamassima*, James introduces Madame de Vionnet as Chad's friend, a figure of sensitivity and paradox. The story of Strether's changes of view about her and Chad, shot through with brilliant images of the beautiful French scene, fascinated readers from the first. In Strether's reported inner thoughts, very occasionally interrupted by the author's qualifications, James's mastery of comic fictional prose is fully evident, as moments of serious aesthetic enjoyment and personal regrets are succeeded by ironic reconsiderations and observations of striking new facts. Strether is a most civilised and engaging American. His refusal to gain anything for himself at the end feels much righter than does Rowland Mallet's ongoing pursuit of Mary Garland. The early reviewers warmed to *The Ambassadors*, regarding it as an elaborate and profound, but not unproblematic, study of American attitudes to life,[33] and James's reputation improved considerably.

There was even an increase in his sales above the six thousand copies per book he could expect. *The Golden Bowl* did well in America, where James's presence as a lecturer aroused much interest. 'The thing has "done" much less ill here than anything I have ever produced',[34] he wrote in 1905, and in the same year he was planning the New York Edition of his novels and tales. The de luxe edition with prefaces outlining the origins of the works was a republishing device known as far back as Scott's time, but it was especially common in the

Edwardian age. The New York Edition (twenty-four volumes, 1907–9, with two more volumes added in 1918, and some important omissions) is, therefore, another witness to James's acute professionalism. It also came out in a limited issue on hand-made paper. Though income from his work was always disappointingly meagre, it was not from want of trying. James employed a literary agent, and was able to finance his travel and larger purchases out of publishers' advances. He took an interest in copyright matters and authors' societies, always acknowledging the commercial context of his composition.[35]

Yet after 1904, James's main work as a novelist was done. The long tour of America in that year and the next bore fruit in *The American Scene* (1907), which is, however, unfinished. He had slowed down considerably. The second volume of the autobiography was less impressive than the first, being eked out with family letters, and the third volume did not get far. There were a few more tales, occasional, rather overblown, essays and an ever-spreading private correspondence, but the evidence of a decline in effectiveness is undeniable. The two novels which, after much labour, he left incomplete at his death, *The Ivory Tower* and *The Sense of the Past*, leave one puzzled as to their ultimate size. Sections of chapters get longer than previous whole chapters, and both fragments spawn working-notes airing the problems posed by the material at such length that James's power of selection is called into doubt. His habit of interminable play with the scenario is symptomatic of chronic indecisiveness. Distractions were seized upon with relief.

Consequently, the role of elderly man of letters came conveniently to James. He put on weight and acted older than he was. Much effort went into conversation, which sometimes approached monologue. He offered advice, too negative to be taken up, to lesser novelists who consulted him. He also had a gift for making others talk; 'marketwomen, tram-conductors, ship-builders, labourers, auctioneers. I have stood by and heard them talk to him for hours. Indeed, I am fairly certain that he once had a murder confessed to him.' Yet despite his psychological insight, he was unsure that he knew the lower-class world.[36] So reported Ford Madox Hueffer, one of many observers who recorded James's appearance and talk. James was on surer ground with the Bloomsbury Group, whose progress he encouraged. In June 1909, he visited Cambridge

and enjoyed seeing Rupert Brooke. Certain of his favourites
wrote appreciative articles about him, such as Sydney Waterlow
and W. Morton Fullerton. A study of *The Novels of Henry James*
by Elizabeth L. Cary appeared in London and New York in
1905, to be followed by Hueffer's *Henry James: A Critical Study*
(1913), where his introduction has James as 'the greatest of
living writers and in consequence, for me, the greatest of living
men'.[37] James sanctioned a selection entitled *The Henry James
Year Book* (1911), introduced by himself and W. D. Howells,
and later authorised extracts for *Pictures and other Passages by
Henry James*, selected by Ruth Head (1916). In 1911, having
attended his brother William's funeral, he received an honorary
degree from Harvard University, in 1912 a D.Litt. from Oxford.
Also in 1912, he gave a lecture on Browning to the Royal
Society of Literature. In 1913 he took a flat in Carlyle Mansions,
Cheyne Walk, Chelsea, for winter residence. He loved this
point of vantage, upstream from the administrative and
commercial capital, and very redolent of Victorian literature.
Here on his seventieth birthday he received a present of a silver
gilt Charles II porringer and dish from nigh upon three hundred
distinguished admirers, from Nancy Astor to Virginia Woolf;
they also commissioned J. S. Sargent to paint his portrait.
James's final accolade was the O.M., announced on the first
day of 1916, two months before his death.

   If the James of these last years was an Establishment figure,
he was by no means universally revered. The charge that he
dealt exclusively with the idle rich and concealed a lack of
substance with a pretentious style surfaced from time to time.
The most wounding attack came late, in 1915, from H. G.
Wells, who, in an exaggerated, rumbustious, almost farcical
way, pilloried James in *Boon*; James ignored ordinary life, he
omitted dreaming, forgetful and whimsical types, and so on. 'It
is a magnificent but painful hippopotamus resolved at any cost,
even at the cost of its dignity, upon picking up a pea which has
got into a corner of its den.'[38] This sort of thing scarcely
deserved to carry much weight: indeed it perversely suggests
James's greatness by its very impatience. James survived it.
The closer political ties between Britain and America before
and during the First World War were working to his advantage.
His position, colossal astride two cultures, rather than
elephantine in any 'den', became a real boon, as the more

prescient in Britain planned a special relationship with their erstwhile colonies, now transformed into a potential superpower.

James gave at times a studied impression of being indifferent to politics. He hated the passions and disturbance aroused by various conflicts, whether in the Sudan or at the hustings. He wrote, for example, in 1884, about his welcome back to London, how he faced 'the British coal-scuttle, the dark back-bedroom, the dim front sitting-room, *The Times*, the hansom-cab, the London dinner, the extension of the franchise, *partagent* my existence. This place *is* hideously political, and there don't seem to me to be three people in it who care for questions of art, or form, or taste. I am lonely and speechless.'[39] But his mood soon altered. Much as he detested the spectacle of politics and war, James was always concerned about power, deceit and human beastliness. He retained a strong sense of the permanent threat of evil, harking back to his grandparents' faith rather than his parents' idealism. As early as 1874 James had pronounced:

> Life *is*, in fact, a battle. On this point optimists and pessimists agree. Evil is insolvent and strong; beauty, enchanting but rare; goodness, very apt to be weak; folly, very apt to be defiant; wickedness, to carry the day; imbeciles to be in great places, people of sense in small, and mankind, generally, unhappy.[40]

Such a well-braced moral outlook, though not desperate, kept James free from illusions most of his life. It did not, however, lead him to favour authoritarian government. He called it rubbish to think of Disraeli as wise or Bismarck as 'a saviour of society'; that was the politics of 'middle-class Toryism and the *Daily Telegraph*'.[41] For his part James stayed sympathetic to the Liberal position. Gladstone amused him with his high-mindedness, but Asquith was a congenial close friend. During the Asquith era it was not unknown for James to dine with Cabinet ministers, including Churchill. Probably it was the fraught first General Election of 1910 which most revealed to him how 'ardent a Liberal' lurked in his own 'cold and clammy exterior'.[42] In 1912 he was turning his attention to the rise of the Left, praising the Liberal Government for 'proceeding very justly, sanely and ably' against Labour in the coal strike: the first country to bring the conflict with Labour, the 'huge Bugaboo', to a practical issue would, he believed, be fortunate.[43] He was also for confronting the much greater menace of military regimes abroad, those 'for the most part raging and would-be throat-cutting and mutually dynamiting nations'[44] which were to provoke the First World War. James's hawkishness in the war sprang from Liberal principles rather than a belligerent temperament. He saw the suppression of Serbia as a cynical abandonment of moral responsibility by Austria–Hungary. He was convinced that Germany had connived at the aggression. There were in Europe insane forces at work, which had been systematically organised and unholily consecrated and which must, after the war, be dealt with, he urged, as a matter of absolute priority.[45] Britain, on the other hand, so assiduous on behalf of peace, was considered by James to have entered the war with a comparatively clean slate. James took this line, which was the orthodox Liberal one, perfectly sincerely.

From August 1914 on, James wanted to have a war-record of his own. His type of war-work consisted in supporting the wounded, caring actively for the refugees and consoling the bereaved. Once, when visiting a hospital, he gave a man who had lost both legs at the Front the will to live, by telling him to try 'to think how all who see you all your life will envy and admire you',[46] a message which was sanguine, possibly, yet apparently effective. James seems to have been trying for a plainer style here. He came to believe that literary style would be changed by the war, which somehow made elaborately expressive effects redundant. He explained during an interview:

> The war has used up words; they have weakened, they have deteriorated like motor-car tyres; they have, during the last six months been, like millions of other things, more overstrained and knocked about and voided of the happy semblance than in all the long ages before and we are now confronted with a depreciation of all our terms, or, otherwise speaking, a loss of expression, through increase of limpness, that may well make us wonder what ghosts will be left to walk.[47]

His own ghost did, of course. He did not live to see the new generation of writers, such as Gertrude Stein or Hemingway, who were to experiment with simpler, less intricate, more abrupt prose than ever he had wanted to write. James's stroke of 2 December 1915 removed his awareness of the war with the same mercy which he himself had shown as a novelist when shifting the point of view from characters whose ordeal of consciousness had become too great for them or us to bear. He lingered for nearly a quarter of a year in Carlyle Mansions, Chelsea, with his mind wandering, sometimes amusingly, and his body partly paralysed. William James's widow came from America to oversee his deterioration and demise. James died on 28 February 1916. His ashes were buried in Cambridge Cemetery, Massachusetts.

Henry James died a British subject. He had been naturalised in 1915, spurred on by the wish to avoid the inconvenience of having to report to the police as an alien in Rye, which was then in a restricted zone. He applied to four persons to be witnesses to his character and profession: they were Asquith, the Prime Minister; Gosse, the Librarian of the House of Lords; George Prothero, the editor of the *Quarterly Review*; and J. B. Pinker, James's literary agent. James gave vent publicly on this occasion to 'his desire to throw his moral weight and personal allegiance, for whatever they may be worth, into the scale of the contending nation's present and future fortune'.[48] Patriotism apart, James could never have anglicised himself. His naturalisation does not allow the English to claim him unequivocally for English literature. But as a symbol of the inter-relationships of the writings of Anglophone peoples and groups all over the world it is a moving and significant act. James seemed also in that pronouncement to be raising, in his modest way, the question of the value of his life's work. To get his novels read and assessed was always his number-one task. He certainly gained some ground, but the battle has had to be won for him, during the last fifty years or so, by his critics.

2

The Victorian James – 'Mme. de Mauves', *The American*, *The Europeans*

James's novels and tales of the 1870s have a remarkable neutrality of tone and an ease in alluding to cultural issues which marked them off as different and new in their day; they were American, certainly, but not folksy or earnest. They lacked the moral sentiment and explicit religious concern which characterised so much nineteenth-century fiction from both sides of the Atlantic. The worlds of work, the poor, the churches, the schools, science and social reform were coolly excluded. It is as if James were inventing a new race of people, bored by all these problems (the sophisticates of the future?), and were assuming that the reader would join them. When James's first volume of fiction was reviewed anonymously, the comment ran: there is a doubt

> whether Mr. James has not too habitually addressed himself less to men and women in their mere humanity, than to a certain kind of cultivated people, who, well as they are in some ways, are often a little narrow in their sympathies and poverty-stricken in the simple emotions.[49]

What is being alluded to here as missing from James is the authorial commitment to good causes and pity for the unfortunate which were associated especially with George Eliot. She, along with James, gives priority to intelligent, amusing analysis, but she wears her heart on her sleeve. James is more distant; it seemed he had moved the novel on to a plane of affluence, American affluence, from which his fictional observers could react to characters and situations in a detached way. The countries of Europe, France, England, Italy and Germany, are for him not the national homes of struggling societies, but the scenes of outdated mannered behaviour. He records social mores as a tourist takes in impressions. In particular in this period there is in James's fiction a satirical attack on French or French-influenced aristocratic behaviour as judged by American democratic, liberal standards. The viewpoint inevitably, then, takes for granted some economic power in the characters: the power to command the resources for travel, language-learning, art-appreciation and leisure. Above all, there is enough money to court the other sex with discrimination, to select sexual partners according to taste. Urbanity prevails, given scope by the absence of urgency over basic needs.

In one sense what is happening is that James is establishing comic conventions for his fiction, setting up genteel Gullivers. The Jamesian observer-figures enable the novelist to contain the melodramatic details of plot, such as adultery, suicide, misdirected passion, duelling and worse, within an ironic framework. But the early James wants to do more than demonstrate his mastery of fictional technique, more than reproduce in an English-language literary context the skills of the French. He has, if not simple values that he wants to put across, an attitude to transmit.

The design which James has on the reader is probably closest in content to that of Matthew Arnold, though James would consider Arnold's explicit encounters with religious and political opponents as being no longer necessary. Arnold's critique of the commercialised ethos and insular prejudices of Britain had deeply impressed James. Through his novels he attempts to gain assent to an Arnoldian critical claim, advocating 'sweetness and light', with a tone that is serene, but mildly ironic, flexibly positive without tendentiousness, questioning various contrasting traditions and concluding lightly without practical recommendations. It is this open-mindedness for which the American money and independence provide uniquely advantageous conditions. James has no need for any other base, whether in Christianity, socialism, science, the classics or art for art's sake.

The effort to produce a new impersonal touch is observable clearly in 'Mme. de Mauves' (*Galaxy*, February–March 1874), the first of these early successes. Though concerned principally with Americans in France, the tale owes more to English writers of the progressive Victorian school, to George Eliot and Arnold, than to any of James's American or French predecessors. The plot concerns an American girl, brought up in France, who marries a French aristocrat out of a romantic enthusiasm for the nobility. Later, disillusioned with her husband over his adulterous inclinations, she falls back on a strict sense of conscience. Conscience compels her both to reject the advances of a very suitable lover, Longmore, and, strangely, to withhold reconciliation from her husband, who commits suicide in disappointment. This sequence of events would probably have been too melodramatic for George Eliot, except for her spells under the influence of George Sand, such as the Laure episode in *Middlemarch* (Chapter XV). *Middlemarch* (1871–2) was, inescapably, freshly present in James's mind when he was writing 'Mme. de Mauves' in 1873. His heroine Euphemia has the George Eliot note, with her 'ardent self-effacement' (iii) and appearance in a vision looking at the frustrated hero 'very gravely and pityingly' (vii). The high-flown conversations of these two, Euphemia and Longmore, sounding of moral virtue and renunciation, have the strained uplift of the *Middlemarch* pair, Dorothea and Ladislaw, except that George Eliot intends marriage for her man. More decisively than George Eliot, James holds himself aloof from Puritan moralism, treating it without tender, nostalgic admiration. Correspondingly he cannot approach her seriousness in the treatment of Lydgate's vocation and marriage, but he can temper his feelings for his characters better. James's calmness of judgment owes much, as I have said, to Matthew Arnold. Indeed we can watch an Arnoldian irony flickering over a George Eliot-type sympathy at the point where Euphemia requests Longmore to leave Paris; any faded compliment on his part, felt Longmore, expired 'before the simple sincerity of her look. She stood there as gently serious as the angel of disinterestedness, and Longmore felt as if he should insult her by treating her words as a bait for flattery' (iv). It is the use of 'disinterestedness' which brings the critical touch to Longmore's response to the heroine's purity. Euphemia's disinterestedness is, in fact, too pure for this world, as Longmore realises when he declines the opportunity to return to her when she is eventually free.

Mme de Mauves' sincerity is not presented as objective or constructive. She relies on the negative principle of conscience, which keeps her as the aggrieved but unerring wife, and Longmore is rebuffed. He thinks she is killing herself with stoicism. She herself admits that her conscience, 'dogged, clinging, inexpungable', will as effectually prevent her from doing anything very fine as anything very base (v). This refusal to 'blaspheme' against conscience aligns Euphemia with many a heroine of Victorian fiction in a moral tradition which goes back through Charlotte Brontë to Bishop Joseph Butler, whose *Fifteen Sermons* (1726) and *Analogy of Religion* (1736) were to be edited by Gladstone. Arnold was to discuss Butler's exposition of the authoritative function of conscience in a tone of nostalgic admiration and reluctant repudiation in his 'Bishop Butler and the Zeit-Geist' (*Contemporary Review*, February/March 1876), having first criticised it as 'vain labour' in a sonnet of 1844.[50] James associates his hero Longmore with this critique of moral absolutism. Here is Longmore meditating on his feelings for a married woman: 'Sacrifice? The word was a trip for minds muddled by fear, an ignoble refuge of weakness. To insist now seemed not to dare, but simply to be, to live on possible terms' (vii). As Longmore begins to question the dictates of his 'Puritanic soul' (iii) and to rebel against the 'lurking principle of asceticism' (vii) which he has in his composition, he is tempted by simple hedonism, by a policy of grasping 'unsparingly at happiness'. This moral shift occurs under the influence of a French artist and his mistress, whom Longmore meets fleetingly at a country inn. This idyllic episode in 'Mme. de Mauves', anticipating the Cheval Blanc scene in *The Ambassadors*, occurs in 'a perfectly rural scene . . . all the French novels seemed to have described it, all the French landscapists to have painted it' (vii). The phrasing, giving priority to art, associates the natural scene, not with transcendence or 'spiritual zeal', but with beauty and 'unperverted reality'. Longmore envies the artist and his poetry-reading companion, identifying himself with the one and Mme de Mauves with the other. The landlady of the inn, however, tells Longmore that the painter changes his companion frequently. Longmore is being too selective in finding parallels with his own situation. The artistic life offers him no solution.

Despite his inner audacity, Longmore remains a

disappointingly obscure figure, a 'modern *bourgeois*', who has less background indicated than anyone else in the tale. Well-off, though not immensely so, handsome, wearing gloves, hat and stick, he is in Europe just to enjoy the paintings, we gather. But he has no artistic vocation of his own and, though he sets down in a notebook 'uncivil jottings' about women and France, he is hardly positive enough to 'write' in the full sense. He is one of a line of Jamesian heroes whose blamelessness is marred by a kind of tentativeness in the presentation, so that, though what he learns is immensely interesting, it could never be said to be a lesson. He is not solid enough for that.

The best thing about 'Mme. de Mauves' is undoubtedly its presentation (this time not at all tentative) of French morals and manners. Much of French life is shown unsparingly as bad, but there is no sense of an unembodied Evil. James had a healthy, horrified respect for the evil in people and society, which he saw as inescapable in our evolutionary condition. He was unable to accept the doctrine of the New England Transcendentalists like Emerson because, as he put it, their 'ripe unconsciousness of evil' was so limiting.[51] The theory of evolution offered, on the other hand, a rational account of sin and wrong, with long-term hope, but no immediate relief. Euphemia's optimistic illusion about the French aristocracy had no excuse really, then; she had derived it from ultramontane fiction in her convent library, but even her own early experience had given her 'a hundred rude hints' against it, which she ignored; and again the De Mauves grandmother, while encouraging the match between Euphemia and Richard de Mauves, had added her warning advice. She told Euphemia not to listen too hard to her own inner voice of conscience, but to treat life more as a game of skill. This advice contradicted itself, since the grandmother was moved by a troubled conscience over her own part in promoting the match. It is Richard who points out this inconsistency to his grandmother, who retires, wounded, to her apartment. To Euphemia he is 'the hero of the young girl's romance made real' (ii), a fatal formula, and the marriage goes ahead. James handles the conflicting scruples and interests of the parties with subtlety; the seeds of the catastrophe are traced and laid bare without exaggerated condemnation.

More cynical is the situation which, later, Longmore faces after the marriage has broken down. He is encouraged by Euphemia's husband and sister-in-law to become her lover so that the husband can all the more conveniently and guiltlessly pursue his own *affaires*. There is no mercenary motive behind this corrupt pressure. It is merely the French propensity to adultery which James has these French characters defending, the right to be bored with and unfaithful to a dutiful wife, especially if she is earnest, middle-class and American. Richard's sister, Mme Clairin, an epigrammatic, 'shrewd Parisienne', is particularly well-conceived by James. We are told that she had married a wholesale druggist for his money, but that he had subsequently gambled away his fortune on the stock-exchange and committed suicide. Hardness and perceptiveness go side-by-side in Mme Clairin's dealings with people. She at first makes advances to Longmore, which he repulses with virtuous horror. She is not without a vindictive streak, and yet is prepared to be generously candid. Her defence of her brother's misconduct shows James's gift for authentic speech already at a peak, highly dramatic, yet also socially illuminating;

'Listen', she went on. 'There has never been a De Mauves who has not given his wife the right to be jealous. We know our history for ages back, and the fact is established. It's a shame if you like, but it's something to have a shame with such a pedigree. The De Mauves are real Frenchmen, and their wives – I may say it – have been worthy of them. You may see all their portraits in our Château de Mauves; everyone of them an "injured" beauty, but not one of them hanging her head. Not one of them had the bad taste to be jealous, . . . These are fine traditions, and it doesn't seem to me fair that a little American *bourgeoise* should come in and interrupt them, and should hang her photograph, with her obstinate little *air penché*, in the gallery of our shrewd fine ladies. A De Mauves must be a De Mauves.

'When she married my brother, I don't suppose she took him for a member of a *société de bonnes oeuvres*. I don't say we're right; who is right? But we're as history has made us, and if anyone is to change, it had better be Mme. de Mauves herself.' (vi)

This self-revealing, yet acutely honest, expression of opinion is condemned by Longmore as superficial and immoral. It is true that Euphemia suffers in this French world, where purity, duty and dignity are daily denied and women may cultivate two jealousies at once, one of a husband and one of a lover. Yet Mme Clairin's view that Euphemia is culpable in 'shutting herself up to read the "imitation"', though biased, expresses a degree of impatience with her which the reader, and eventually Longmore, shares. James is even able, while maintaining his reservations, to swing sympathy round towards the erring French husband. James can be credited with having moved on now from simple conflicts between rectitude and sin, good and evil, to imaginative comedy. Despite its heaviness of phrase, 'Mme. de Mauves' is a deeply amusing work, liberally progressive in its assumptions, building on the idea of moral conflict which it analyses.

James reconstituted the elements of his fictional French nobility, with some additions, for *The American* (*Atlantic Monthly*, June 1876 to May 1877), his third novel. Here, however, the representative family, the Bellegardes, is not cynically permissive, but hidebound by honour; they are negative in their reactions to the American intruder. There is no protective grandmother or witty seductress, but rather a mixed gallery of legitimist diehards and weak conformists concealing a family crime. *The American*, as the title promises, also features a distinct national type as its hero, the rich but inexperienced businessman, Newman, searching for culture and a wife among the denizens of the Old World. The meeting of these extremes ends messily. There is no character sufficiently calm or detached to fix the significance. The nearest to a sophisticated commentator is Mrs Tristram, Newman's confidante in Paris, a humorous American expatriate dissatisfied with her own marriage, who is, however, mischievously sanguine about the outcome of Newman's quest. Speaking, for example, of her school-friend Claire de Bellegarde, now the widowed Mme de Cintré, she says:

'when I left the convent she had to give me up. I was not of her *monde*; I am not now, either, but we sometimes meet. They are terrible people – her *monde*; all mounted upon stilts a mile high, and with pedigrees long in proportion. It is the skim of the milk of the old *noblesse*. Do you know what a

Legitimist is, or an Ultramontane? Go into Madame de
Cintré's drawing-room some afternoon, at five o'clock, and
you will see the best-preserved specimens. I say go, but no
one is admitted who can't show his fifty quarterings.'
   'And this is the lady you propose to me to marry?' asked
Newman. 'A lady I can't even approach?'
   'But you said just now that you recognised no obstacles.'
(Chapter III)

James's mode here is comic exaggeration. It is also applied to
Newman himself. There is a lot of such amusing writing in the
long build-up to the rejection of Newman by Claire's mother
and brother (Chapter XVIII), but then the pitch falters. There
is an unusual lack of verve in the last third of *The American*.
Compare James's successful, if simple, use of suspense in the
snatch of conversation just quoted with his reliance on
melodramatic routine in the following (from Chapter XXII): it
concerns certain secret details contained in the letter in which
the elder Henri-Urbain de Bellegarde had accused his wife
(Claire's mother) of attempting to murder him:

   'I can't tell you, sir', answered Mrs. Bread. 'I couldn't
read it; it was in French.'
   'But could no one else read it?'
   'I never asked a human creature.'
   'No one has ever seen it?'
   'If you see it you'll be the first.'
   Newman seized the old woman's hand in both his own and
pressed it vigorously. 'I thank you ever so much for that', he
cried, 'I want to be the first; I want it to be my property and
no one else's! You're the wisest old woman in Europe. And
what did you do with the paper?' This information had made
him feel extraordinarily strong. 'Give it to me quick!'
   Mrs. Bread got up with a certain majesty. 'It is not so easy
as that, sir. If you want the paper you must wait.'
   'But waiting is horrible, you know', urged Newman.
   'I am sure *I* have waited these many years', said Mrs.
Bread.

Waiting of this sort certainly is horrible. The very fact that
James could call a character 'Mrs. Bread' betokens some
temporary loss of wit (his English characters of this period are

usually stuffy). The passage seems ripe for conversion into bad
drama. It reminds us what a poor showing James made on the
Victorian stage, for which the play-version of *The American* was
for years his main hope. The bones of Plot seem to require from
him, as here, a sagging, limp covering of conventional
expressions. The whole device of the admonitory waiting-
woman who has the power to turn the tables on the formidable
Bellegardes is ill-judged. James was betrayed by his wish to fill
out the novel with explicit incidents – a dual, death-bed
confession, sick-bed crime, convent-interview, renunciation of
revenge – set in romantic, almost operatic, scenery. The writing
sinks to an appropriate level. There is a lift only at the very end
when the letter is burned and the reappearance of the arch Mrs
Tristram brings some echoes of the earlier exchanges.

Fortunately, in a way, none of this stagey action is necessary
to the main point of *The American*, which is the mutual
incomprehensibility of Newman and the Bellegardes, their
inability to stomach him as an in-law and his perplexity over
Claire's decision to take the veil. The revelation of these states
of mind form the true climax of the novel; both are
characteristically Jamesian, ambiguous and negative. The
Bellegardes' sacrifice of Newman's money on an issue of taste
later struck James himself as implausible; in reality, such a
family would have 'jumped'[52] at a rich American, he came to
believe. Yet a theme of merely hypocritical mercenariness would
surely have reduced the stronger, earlier part of the novel to the
level of the rest. As it is, the Bellegardes are an interestingly
outlined family-group, tempted by Newman's wealth, but not
able to live with him. Only the mother wields true authority,
and all the others temporise, while her judgment is suspended.
The tension gives rise to some electrifying scenes in which
Newman's good nature rubs against the impenetrable exterior
of the French characters. The pleasure which this part of *The
American* gives the reader is not particularly dependent on
recognition of ideas of culture, society or psychology but tends
to be fairly elementary. The emphasis is all foregrounded on
the struggle for advantage. None of the main French characters
is presented from within. Mme de Cintré's acceptance of
Newman's proposal of marriage is, therefore, a surprise, coming
after so much reticence and delay. The scene in which the news
bursts has a grim humour, with the clash of wills issuing in

cryptic dialogues of a kind that sometimes anticipates I. Compton-Burnett:

> 'I congratulate you, sir', said Madame de Bellegarde, with extreme solemnity. 'My daughter is an extraordinarily good woman. She may have faults, but I don't know them.'
>   'My mother does not often make jokes,' said Madame de Cintré; 'but when she does they are terrible.'
>   . . . The marquis stood looking for awhile into the crown of his hat. 'We have been prepared', he said at last, 'but it is inevitable that in the face of the event one should experience a certain emotion'. And he gave a most unhilarious smile.
>   'I feel no emotion that I was not perfectly prepared for', said his mother. (Chapter XIV)

It is at this very point, we later discover, that Claire's mother and brother decide against Newman, though all we are aware of at the time is the sinister surface. The style is now nearer to tragedy than comedy, but there is no sense of inevitability, for the Bellegardes do Newman what justice they can. Claire loves him up to a point, and would like to come up to the high mark of his womanly ideal, which is 'better' then her own. But her own ideal of obedience to the authority of the family and the church apparently prevails. One supposes it must be Newman's homely complacency – 'I feel quite like one of the family' (Chapter XVI) – that provokes the Bellegardes to reject him. Whatever the motivation, the Bellegardes have a two-dimensional power to hold the reader's attention which persists for much of the novel.

Possibly Newman is all the better for lacking the type of intelligence which could have prevented his disappointment. His unawareness of the codes of an orthodox, authoritarian social order and their underlying abuses is a kind of innocence. We are told that the highest uses of intelligence known to Newman 'were transcendent sagacities in the handling of railway stock' (Chapter XVII). James's choice of words here suggests a dichotomy in American life between Emerson-type idealism and the mechanism of capitalism, but Newman seems to embody both strands in American culture unwittingly. James's attitude to Newman is warm, without socialist bitterness, respectful of egalitarian frankness, but not entirely coherent.

America was too complex to be represented by one figure, 'The American'. Newman is sometimes narrow, sometimes generous. Alongside his undiscriminating amiability there is also a moral censoriousness. James uses him both as an object (American quaintness) and as a subject (the vehicle for a critique of French *moeurs*). For example, Mlle Nioche, the *femme du monde* type, who makes a career out of being the mistress of rich men, driven there partly by her father's need of financial support, is at first comically mistaken by Newman for a genuine artist, but later angrily condemned as a predatory opportunist or prostitute. Again, young Mme de Bellegarde, Claire's sister-in-law, whose dream is to dance at the Bal Bullier in the Latin quarter, 'where the students dance with their mistresses', is marked down by Newman as an heiress of noble traditions aspiring merely to witness 'a couple of hundred young ladies kicking off young men's hats' (Chapter XVII). The prim disapproval of vulgar Parisian entertainments is in line with Arnold's deploring of the French worship of the 'great goddess Lubricity'[53]; it goes beyond being an observation upon the young Marquise's boredom, and teeters awkwardly between delicacy and indelicacy.

The American side of *The American* is somewhat blurred, then. Newman is conceived as a doer, a self-made businessman, carrying in his head a stereotyped image of the desirable, elegant wife, but he is also used as a sensitive observer, a moraliser who hasn't time to moralise, capable of tender protectiveness and caring for something above bargains. The difficulty is felt in a phrase which James applies to him, 'there is sometimes nothing like the imagination of those people who have none' (Chapter V), where the paradox is not deep but unresolvable. Mere contrast or discontinuity in a fictional character is not necessarily a weakness; it may have a functional role, if it is seen as socially conditioned, signifying contradictions in the society which produced it. But Newman's presence in *The American* is too pervasive to be so reduced. He himself is made to comment disarmingly on the different interpretations of his own character in his letter from Baden-Baden to Mrs Tristram. He had been told by a Unitarian minister from Boston that he was 'a devotee of "art for art" – whatever that is' and then by a London journalist that he was 'too virtuous by half; I was too stern a moralist. . . . This was rather bewildering.

Which of my two critics was I to believe?' There is, of course,
more to the problem than the Hellenist-Hebraist polarity which
he proposes here. Newman is a backwoodsman, only learning
Arnoldian roles such as those two suggested. But James found
the pioneering, frontier-moving, fortune-amassing elements in
American history uncongenial. He seems to have constructed
this part of Newman's experience from books with which he
was not entirely at ease. When we are told that if Newman had
met Valentin de Bellegarde 'on a Western prairie he would
have felt it proper to address him with a "How-d'ye-do,
Mosseer?"' and that he felt towards Valentin the same kindness
that he 'used to feel in his earlier years for those of his
companions who could perform strange and clever tricks –
make their joints crack in queer places or whistle at the back of
their mouths' (Chapter VII), we seem momentarily to be in a
more robust world altogether, that, say, of Mark Twain's 'Jim
Smiley and his Jumping Frog' (*Saturday Press*, New York, 18
November 1865). It is not that a Western Newman could not
serve James a turn, terribly derived though he might seem, but
that he cannot serve linguistically the subtle turns that *The
American* actually requires of him. When Newman insists upon
saving Mme de Cintré from the extravagance of her own
generosity or finds her decision 'to snuffle herself in ascetic rags'
a 'confounding combination of the inexorable and the grotesque'
(Chapter XX), he seems to have brought his integrity maybe,
but not his words and thoughts any more, from the West. F. R.
Leavis goes as far as to call James's idealisation of Newman
'romantic, unreal and ridiculous'.[54] The problem arises from
James's choice of so unfamiliar, unrooted a type as both subject
and object, as a vehicle for sophisticated observation and as
someone who is peculiarly limited. The problems posed in *The
American* by the dubious status of the hero and the melodramatic
nature of the plot are solved in subsequent novels in various
ways; partly by making the observer-figure literary, young or
female and partly by confining the sensational interpretation of
the incidents to minor characters given to exaggerating
everything.

The Europeans (1878), the obverse of *The American*, is James's
first sure success. Though planned fairly lightly and executed
swiftly, it engaged James at a profound level with felicitous
results. Its subject, the quiet New England Puritan tradition on

the point of attenuation, was one which he viewed with genuine
affection and respect. He was able, therefore, to treat it with
unembarrassed irony and complex, secure criticism. The more
dubious European sophisticates are here the travelling observers,
brother and sister, talented, but not rich, and the America
which they encounter has the true strangeness of the New
World. Though the commercial prosperity of the Wentworths
and their connections is not left unexplained by James, the
predominant note of *The Europeans* is pastoral. As Felix Young
puts it on arrival:

> It's intensely rural, tremendously natural; and all overhung
> with this strange white light, this far-away blue sky. . . . I
> should say there was wealth without symptoms. A plain,
> homely way of life; nothing for show, and very little for –
> what shall I call it? – for the senses; but a great *aisance*, and a
> lot of money, out of sight, that comes forward very quietly for
> subscriptions to institutions, for repairing tenements, for
> paying doctors' bills; perhaps even for portioning daughters.
> (Chapter III)

Felix's tone here towards his sister Eugenia, the Baroness
Münster, is all that James needs to open the European
perspective on old New England. We note the social *savoir-faire*
evident in the use of the French word, the artistic priority, the
scrupulous deployment of wit and paradox. Though their first
appearance is as fortune-hunters, Felix and his sister prove in
the end to be less mercenary than expected. Felix marries
Gertrude Wentworth genuinely for love, not for her dowry, and
Eugenia graciously retires empty-handed without trying too
many ploys. Though Felix adapts easily to the carefree life, he
is not entirely admirable. A natural optimist, he is represented
as abandoning a mild form of Bohemianism for the 'profession'
of hack portrait-painting. He thinks his commitment to earning
his living with his brush will win his prospective New England
father-in-law's good will: 'I find I can earn my living – a very
fair one – by going about the world and painting bad portraits.
It's not a glorious profession, but it's a perfectly respectable
one. You won't deny that, eh?' he asks Mr Wentworth, and
then continues with his stream of disarming, slightly shocking
self-justification and apology, which induces in the older man 'a

period of severe reticence' (Chapter XII). It is almost certain that George Eliot and G. H. Lewes did not like *The Europeans*,[55] and this uncondemning presentation of Felix, the irrepressible, unearnest, lightly responsible artist and husband, explains why. Felix does not suffer enough – on the contrary he amuses himself too much – to earn or deserve Gertrude Wentworth according to the ethic of self-denial. The critique of his character is subtle; it is found not so much in authorial comment, but in his own self-revelation or in the hint that his sister is bored by his continual good humour. Actually, in assuming what Mr Wentworth is feeling about his proposal, Felix is wide of the mark. It is not his want of means that troubles his host so much as his want of understanding of Christian doctrine. Mr Brand, of course, has the required amount of that. When Mr Brand insists on the marriage of Felix and Gertrude, Mr Wentworth waives his objection. He entrusts his conscience to the young minister, who, however, is principally engaged in returning one good turn for another, since Felix had put him in the way of Gertrude's sister, Charlotte.

The Europeans is full of such comic misunderstandings, reverses of expectation, words taken the wrong way, uninformed questioning, ill-matched pairing of characters, leading, amazingly, to wedding-bells, sound marriages and family reconciliation. Yet this novel is not purely a comedy. The Baroness Münster remains an unfulfilled, dissatisfied figure. The final revelation that the New Englander whom she had hoped to catch, Robert Acton, 'after his mother's death, married a particularly nice young girl', provides the novel with a memorable sting in the tail. It is the first of James's ironical last sentences. The happy turn of events (for Robert) neatly robs the novel of its happy ending. Eugenia, for all her faults, deserved not to have to return to the world of forced and failed human relationships symbolised by the court of Siberstadt-Schreckenstein. She has no chance of marrying a particularly nice young man, nor will anybody prompt her thoughts in favour of another party who is unknowingly in love with her as Felix and Gertrude do for Charlotte and Mr Brand. There are reminders of Shakespearian comedy in *The Europeans*, especially of *Much Ado About Nothing*, and, appropriately enough, the 'capital mixture' (Chapter X) of perplexity and enchantment, which Mr Brand feels, no more extends to all the characters than it does in the Shakespeare. But the exclusion of Eugenia from the felicity is sharper than we expect from her generally comic role. Inadvertently, her visit to New England precipitates marriages between others rather than conducing to one of her own. Her fascinating personality, with her cultivation of elegant manners, fashionable decor and *risqué* repartee, covers a very unromantic predicament. No one but James could have imagined such a figure in America or kept it consistent.

Enough of Eugenia's European background is sketched in for James's purpose. We know that she is married morganatically to the younger brother of the Reigning Prince of a 'perfectly despotic little state' in pre-Bismarck Germany. We also learn that the Prince plans a political second marriage for Eugenia's husband, who, despite being a 'ninny' (Chapter II), might yet defy his brother and keep Eugenia on. A less ingenious novelist might have risked a Ruritanian first chapter, in which Eugenia's problems and the petty intrigues of Silberstadt-Schreckenstein were highlighted. But James wanted the courtly European world presented through American eyes, those of the romantic Gertrude and the morally suspicious Mr Wentworth. Eugenia carries enough of Europe with her in her airs and graces, her discretion and pathos, to convey its curiosity value which she scarcely appreciates. As a woman of middle-class American origin attached to aristocratic values she has a double function for James: to illustrate the faltering uncertainty of the old regime confronted with a challenge from the capitalist society of America and to reflect the limited security offered to a woman in the Old World as compared with precarious, illusory independence available to her in the New. These roles are complementary.

It is significant that Felix rarely knows how to take his sister, being unsure of her reactions and afraid of her occasional hardness and perversity. Eugenia is always betraying her uncertainty of purpose. When introduced to Mr Brand, she makes a gaffe by commenting on his Unitarianism as 'Something new' (Chapter III), bestowing only a glance upon him before studying the eligible Robert Acton. Her performance is *too* calculating for her to anticipate its effects. The youngest couple, Lizzie Acton and Clifford Wentworth, soon start reacting against her. Eugenia's efforts, undertaken in compliance with Felix's plan, to smooth away the rough edges of Clifford's personality by receiving him as if he were a young Frenchman attached to an older woman, put her in a false position. She precipitates Clifford's marriage with Lizzie: 'I am certainly very stupid not to have thought of that' (Chapter XII), arousing hostility in the sister of the man she hopes to marry, as well as in her uncle. She does not find the fortune which she had sought in America; 'conditions of action on this provincial continent were not favourable to really superior women. The elder world was after all their natural field' (Chapter XII). Gertrude Wentworth would agree, but the biological metaphor is shot through with irony. Neither 'provincial' nor 'elder' here is a scientific term; both are cultural ones. Eugenia's superiority is not to be taken for granted. The real point is that the Baroness Münster proves unadaptable and her Europe of small states is obsolete.

Eugenia is wrong to assume that the Americans in the novel have no standard of comparison with her 'remarkable self' (Chapter IV) and that they will therefore be unable to discover anything against her. Robert Acton, a university man of considerable experience in business, travel and reading, is vigilantly observant. The scene in which she discusses with him her possible courses of action with regard to her marriage is one of the best in *The Europeans*. She has been driven in Acton's high wagon to a Massachusetts beauty-spot, where, conveniently, a 'rustic wayfarer' holds Acton's two horses, a 'service he consented to render, as a friendly turn to a fellow-citizen'; no money changes hands. The wildness of the scenery adds something, we are told, to Eugenia's 'sense of the enlargement of opportunity which had been born of her arrival in the New World' (Chapter VI). James is deliberately presenting a much more favourable view of American openness than Dickens had done in *Martin Chuzzlewit* (1843), where the emphasis is all on dollars, fraud and swamps. Eugenia finds herself in a world that is republican, romantic, free for development. Her response, however, is to hope for service; she feels that Acton is a companion who 'would do a great many things that she might ask him'. She sees opportunity too much as a preservation of privilege. Eugenia's visit to the Actons' house, which follows immediately after the dialogue in the country, is marred by her dislike of Lizzie, whose combination of 'a taste for housework and the wearing of fresh, Parisian-looking dresses suggested the possession of a dangerous energy' (Chapter VI). Style and labour must be separate, as far as Eugenia is concerned, yet Lizzie, for all her rawness and pertness, is felt to have the advantage. Then when Eugenia meets Mrs Acton, an invalid of whom her son hardly ever speaks (her delicate maternal presence had resolved itself, as James finely put it, perhaps thinking of his own mother, 'simply into the subjective emotion of gratitude'), she puts her foot in it. 'He has talked to me immensely of you. Oh, he talks of you as you would like . . . as such a son *must* talk of such a mother' (Chapter VI). Eugenia proceeds by a formula of compliment, meaning no harm. But the New Englanders prefer modesty and honesty. The fact that Eugenia applies European social routines to a private American situation tells against her. Yet she has some grounds to be annoyed with the Actons for disapproving of her just for telling a white lie. The episode, with its anger, failure of communication, moral impasse, is both amusing and sad. It has the winsome note which is also found in the subtlest scenes in Tolstoy.

Balanced against the Baroness's somewhat enervated view of things is Felix's un-self-reproachful hedonism, which is, despite the lack of moral gravity, associated by James with a love of the arts such as he had inherited from his own New York upbringing. Felix has lived by playing the violin and acting Shakespeare in various European countries, as well as by painting. Felix's visual sense dovetails neatly with his moral sense in his delight at the ease of contact with young girls which America's freer society affords him; in his previous relations with virtuous unmarried gentlewomen, as it now seemed to him, 'he had been looking at pictures under glass', but the American girls

> were always in the right light. He liked everything about them: he was, for instance, not at all above liking the fact that they had very slender feet and high insteps. He liked their pretty noses; he liked their surprised eyes and their hesitating, not at all positive way of speaking; he liked so much knowing that he was perfectly at liberty to be alone for hours, anywhere, with either of them . . . (Chapter IV)

James's precise, yet politely metaphoric prose traces the stages by which Felix moves from the aesthetic to the physical, to the cultural-social and finally to the personal-sexual, as he begins to distinguish his feelings for Gertrude as stronger. Felix seems to combine the Arnoldian advantages of a Hellenist play of mind with a Hebraic restraint of conduct. The association of the aesthetic tendency with a power of moral discovery works on us in his favour. He worries lest his courting of Gertrude Wentworth is an offence against her father's hospitality towards his sister and himself, as it would be in Europe, but Mr Wentworth never thinks of such a thing. American egalitarianism extends to the treatment of the young. Mr Wentworth's statement to Gertrude, 'We are all princes here' (Chapter IV), has in the end to apply to Gertrude herself, despite his reservations about her character. Mr Wentworth's conscientiousness is too negative and rigid, no doubt, too embarrassed and surprised by frankness about sex and religion. Gertrude feels it as repressive. She rebels against her family and circle of friends, who, she feels, try to make her feel guilty. Felix is delighted to be her rescuer, yet there is something hard in her determination to escape to what she thinks is Bohemia.[56] Her willingness to emulate Eugenia's manner is surely misplaced; 'she wished that – to give her the charm – she might in future very often be bored' (Chapter XI). One can see that Gertrude's lack of concern with the great moral problems is in danger of being more than temperamental. She analyses Mr Brand's motive of self-exaltation for his offer of performing the marriage-ceremony with almost chilling clarity. But there is no suggestion that Felix does not respect Gertrude's determination to use the freedom which is her birthright or that their marriage will not be one of mutual support and correction.

The Europeans, then, achieves an almost perfect blend of seriousness and irony in dramatising James's pre-occupations in the 1870s, the age of high Darwinism and secularism. Though set back in the 1840s, it handles essentially contemporary issues: the infringement of democratic attitudes on authoritarian social codes, and *vice versa*;[57] the evolution of morality from reliance on religious dogma to trust in imaginative experience, fostered by the arts; and the importance of international contact and understanding. At the same time, in the figure of Gertrude Wentworth *The Europeans* poses a question which was to dominate the next phase of James's fiction – what is the position of American women?

3

American Girls – 'Daisy Miller', 'The Pension Beaurepas', *Washington Square, The Portrait of a Lady*

There is an impressive range of women-characters in James's fiction. Drawn to the world of wealth and leisure as a subject, a world which was at the same time, ironically, the context for his own hermetic labours as a writer, James perhaps inevitably came to concentrate on the feminine. Correspondingly, most of his male characters seem to be concentrating on women too.

There is a precedent in Hawthorne. James already knew Hawthorne's novels well before re-reading them for his critical study *Hawthorne* (1879). Undoubtedly James was influenced by a structural feature of Hawthorne's stories, the pairing of different American females types: there is the religious innocent turning away from guilt and evil and the cultured idealist entangling herself in romantic passion.[58] Mary Garland in *Roderick Hudson* has much in common with the first and various James characters suggest aspects of the second.

James, however, belonging to a more emancipated age, was less interested than Hawthorne in the conditions of sin, crime and personal obsession; he addressed himself to what was in some ways a more normal world of money, art-appreciation, expanding professions, current affairs, international understanding. Morality in James is now more a matter of questions and scruples than imperatives, though he is also increasingly concerned with individual terror and horror as psychological problems. Around 1880, the women in James's fiction seem only on the verge of recognising their sexuality or determining a

44

political role for themselves. But, though not able to vote, they are frequently critical of the men, sceptical of authoritarian traditions and prepared to exercise, and sometimes to exaggerate, what freedom they in fact have. These middle-class American women are rarely explicit Christians or reckless lovers, but usually conscientious, culturally curious seekers of influence and exponents of independence. They reflect and carry forward the three main intellectual traditions affecting nineteenth-century America – Puritan restraint, Enlightenment rationality and Romantic individualism.

At the same time they have usually left America for Europe. James was dissatisfied with other nineteenth-century American developments like democratic rowdiness, excessive commercialism, ostentatious expenditure and sensational publicity. James observed the effects of class mobility on the women of the Gilded Age: their crudity of taste and manners and the separation of the sexes, the men getting, the women spending, the rapidly amassed fortunes. Certain of his female characters come from small-town backgrounds, flaunting wealth or seeking rank; others display provincial ignorance of the done thing, but maintain a classless openness and willingness to be natural. Radicalness might mean different things at this period in Boston, London and Paris, as is clear from the discussion in Chapter XXVIII of *The Portrait of a Lady* (when, ten chapters later, we read that Ralph Touchett calls Lord Warburton 'the head of the Communists', we can hardly believe our eyes, and James himself revised the phrase). But it is clear that after the abolition of slavery and the end of the Civil War, the fairer treatment of women became the most contentious reformist issue in American politics. James saw the potential of this change in social attitudes for both comedy and pathos in his fiction. Indeed his fiction was ahead in this respect, and contributed to the change.

'Daisy Miller' (*Cornhill Magazine*, June–July 1878) was James's first real success, bringing him more celebrity than any other of his works. Not only, in his own words, did it make 'a great hit'[59] in England: it also, according to W. D. Howells, divided America, where James's female readership 'resented while it adored his portraits of American women'.[60] That the tale has a quality deeper than the controversy which its heroine's audacity aroused is suggested by the fact that Leslie Stephen (no populist) accepted it for publication 'with effusion'.[61] James based the tale on actual incidents which had been related to him in 1877.[62] He wrote it quickly, interrupting work on *The Europeans*, which he finished later. It seems that James was subject to exceptional imaginative pressure over 'Daisy Miller'. The Preface to the New York edition admits as much, referring to the 'poetical terms' in which the 'little exhibition' is made.[63] Seeing her primarily as an example of the American girl unprepared for life, 'as the European order expressed life', without any sense of responsibility or reciprocity, James nevertheless believed that Daisy Miller's 'negatives were converted and became in certain relations lively positives and values'.[64] The negatives are a flatness due to a lack of inner culture, a disposition to blunder about matters of information, an incaution in making new acquaintances and a defiance of the climate, which are transformed by youthful beauty and natural vivacity into unsnobbish simplicity, spontaneity, trustfulness and a love of activity. The absence of cynicism and neglect of 'form' give Daisy Miller a poignant quality, 'a shy incongruous charm', for which James evidently felt 'a sufficiently brooding tenderness'.[65] The sub-title 'A Study' may raise expectations of extended, sociological commentary rather than sensitive concern. But the story's very shortness is part of its appeal; far from implying slightness of significance, it makes the removal of the heroine from the scene of life more touching. Unlike his Victorian predecessors, James hardly ever goes wrong with death, and the guarded pathos with which he handles Daisy Miller's succumbing to malaria is just right.

Sentimentality (and facility of assessment too) is excluded from 'Daisy Miller' by James's use of figural narration; that is, the narrator privileges the point of view of one figure, Frederick Winterbourne. The other characters – Daisy Miller, her muddled mother, her spoilt young brother, the Italians, the disapproving older confidantes – are all seen through Winterbourne's eyes. The narrator himself merely has a few things to say about the locations and about Winterbourne's other interests. We are told that Winterbourne has been a student in Geneva, but whether he still is, or his main preoccupation there is an older foreign woman, we never find out. Since the narrator knows Winterbourne's detailed reactions every time he encounters Daisy Miller, it is disconcerting that he knows nothing of his thoughts about the other woman. Winterbourne never compares the two. Instead he denies the rival's existence. Yet James has him wonder at the rapidity of Daisy's induction that there was a charmer in Geneva who was keeping him in thrall. Contradictory accounts of Winterbourne's 'motive of sojourn' in Geneva conclude the tale: 'a report that he is "studying" hard – an intimation that he is much interested in a very clever foreign lady'. Both accounts are acceptable. Winterbourne is presented as both learned and sexually confident ('"My dear aunt, I am not so innocent", said Winterbourne, smiling and curling his moustache.') The discontinuity in the dramatisation of consciousness is deliberate on James's part, since the learning blocks the sexuality in the case of Winterbourne's relationship with Daisy Miller. 'I never saw a man that knew so much!' she exclaims. This lack of sophistication defeats him. The reader is left in the dark about Winterbourne on vital matters just as Daisy is, and so indirectly identifies with her, in spite of everything that tells against her.

Winterbourne does, as his aunt predicts, make a mistake over Daisy Miller. He accepts Daisy's invitation to come on from Vevey to Rome specifically for her and not for his aunt, but then holds off because she seems to be acting like a dangerous flirt and trying to make him jealous by associating with Giovanelli, the 'little Italian'. Winterbourne has been away from America too long to know 'where he is' with Daisy Miller's good nature. The mistake was not to realise that she would have appreciated his respect.

Daisy Miller does not, of course, act out of caprice or the desire to shock. She innocently ignores social conventions, conventions observed in the higher echelons of New York society as well as in Europe. She comes from Schenectady, upstate; and Mrs Miller is quite unfearful of social disapproval in allowing her daughter to enjoy gentlemen's company. Daisy simply wishes to exercise her right to choose what male companions she pleases, without prejudice or suspicion. Friendly warnings are of no avail. She does not want to know what people may be saying about her, as she would not like what they meant. She treats Giovanelli fondly, but without commitment. She does not want to use love as a means to gain. Winterbourne's comment to his aunt on this point has a finely cutting irony: 'Daisy and her mamma have not yet risen to that

stage of – what shall I call it? – of culture, at which the idea of
catching a count or a *marchese* begins. I believe that they are
intellectually incapable of that conception'. Winterbourne's bias
makes him associate thought with moral pessimism; he does
not recognise that the Millers' background includes a rival
intellectual system which they cannot formulate or defend, but
which is part of the American experience, Emersonian,
Romantic, Rousseau-esque. Daisy Miller has a liking for
natural, kind, open people. She perceives, as if by instinct (but
it is how she has been brought up), that Winterbourne is too
stiff and quaint, though the width of his knowledge is admirable.
She understands that Giovanelli is not the gigolo or fortune-
hunter that Winterbourne jadedly assumes him to be, but is a
decent man who knows he has very little hope of marrying her.
She thinks it *natural* to introduce such gentleman-friends to her
mother. Why not? She is better-mannered than her hostess at
Mrs Walker's party, even if she does talk through the music. As
James explained privately, 'The whole idea of the story is the
little tragedy of a light, thin, natural, unsuspecting creature
being sacrificed as it were to a social rumpus that went on quite
over her head and to which she stood in no measureable
relation.'[66] Her relation to the idea of nature is measurable
enough, however. Daisy Miller acts as they do in Schenectady
without being articulate on the reasons for freer patterns of
behaviour. She carries the virtues as well as the defects of the
New World abroad.

Against this point in her favour have to be set her naievity
and insouciance, which so amuse and dismay Winterbourne.
She expects him as a matter of course to know various people
whom she has met by chance on her European travels. She has
no idea how to discipline the pert Randolph, who 'in a manner'
introduces Winterbourne to his sister, with unintended irony,
as 'an American man'. But it is in the matter of her own health
and safety that Daisy Miller is most vulnerable. Mrs Miller's
hapless concern here has a premonitory quality. There is a cold
tinge (reflected in Winterbourne's name) to the comic dialogue
where the mother's worry over Daisy's physical exertions is
mistaken by Winterbourne for worry over etiquette ('It seems
as if there was nothing she wouldn't undertake'). His reflection
that Mrs Miller's was a 'very different type of maternity from
that of the vigilant matrons' of Geneva shows his latent

sensitivity. But Daisy Miller's actual exposure to malaria in the early Roman spring defeats everybody.[67] She insists on seeing the Colosseum by moonlight, declaring, 'I never was sick, and I don't mean to be!' She adds, 'in a strange tone', that she does not care if she has Roman fever or not. It may be that her indifference is due to a feeling of disappointment over Winterbourne. She sees that people are being unkind to her in giving her 'the cold shoulder'. Liberty is a dangerous weapon to use in a state of depression. Yet neither the heroine's incompetence nor society's rough handling of her gives rise to disproportionate bitterness in the reader. James plays tactfully with both our alarm and our affection.

James was eager to refute the suggestion that the Millers were his version of typical Americans abroad. They have a crassness which is not found in Bessie Alden in 'An International Episode' (*Cornhill Magazine*, December 1878 – January 1879). Here the American girl, while visiting England to renew acquaintance with Lord Lambeth, coolly rejects his proposal of marriage, not only because of the overbearing attitude of his relatives, but also because he does not share her own interest in literature, history and politics. But in 'The Pension Beaurepas' (*Atlantic Monthly*, April 1879) James returned to the attack with a story which involves two kinds of Americans abroad in the one place. The types had already been distinguished in his 'Americans Abroad', an essay of October 1878, as those who, finding life at home disagreeable, spend years in Europe 'trying to get into society' and those who, lacking social standing at home, look on foreign travel as a reward for their 'sordid toil'.[68] The first group is represented in 'The Pension Beaurepas' by the German-reading Mrs Church and her daughter Aurora, who envies the 'absolute liberty' of young girls back in Boston; the second by the bemused businessman Mr Ruck and his materialistic wife and daughter, who are intent only on acquiring jewelry, clothes and lace as trophies of the trip. James recognised in the Preface to the New York edition that the Rucks' situation was one that could 'freely recur', for the tale is built on the contrast between 'the distinctively American and the distinctively European outlook'.[69] Indeed it belies James's assertion that he was 'helpless' in responding to the mystery of 'the American business-man' and unable to take on elder American women as characters because of their 'inveterate blankness of surface'.[70]

He finds ways to take on both. He puts them in conflict and he has them observed from various points of view.

The *presentation* of the characters is particularly felicitous in 'The Pension Beaurepas'. James, remembering that it was in Geneva that he made his own first literary efforts, uses as a first-person narrator an unattached American of good family with 'a fancy for a literary career' (i). His powers of description are, therefore, appropriately exercised on the people and the place; at the same time he is too young to share Mr Ruck's business-knowledge or to respond ambiguously (like Winterbourne) to American girls' initiatives. He reports also the views of two elderly Swiss characters, Madame Beaurepas, the owner of the pension, and Monsieur Pigeonneau, from Lausanne (but self-styled a Frenchman, late of Paris), who has 'broken his fall' as a guest in the pension (ii). Madame Beaurepas supplies the experience which the narrator lacks, readily classifying people and predicting the course of events. She actually prefers the Rucks to the Churches as more likely to pay their way and not to fuss; 'The line of misconduct to which she most objected was an undue assumption of gentility; she had not patience with boarders who gave themselves airs' (i). James utilises this shrewd observer to sketch future melodramatic developments which the tale itself eschews: she foresees that Aurora Church, tired of her mother's attempts to 'marry' her, will one day elope with a young American, a less reasonable type than the narrator; 'She wishes to *courir les champs*' (vi). Similarly fancifully, Monsieur Pigeonneau supplies the love-interest. He considers himself an expert on female form, recommending the narrator to take up with Mrs Ruck; 'I like those large, fair, quiet women; they are often, *dans l'intimité*, the most agreeable' (iv). He has the bawdiest turn of any James character.

Mrs Church swoops to rescue her daughter not only from his delightful company but also from the unstuffy Sophy Ruck, whose rough tongue and vital Philistinism are not without their fascination. Aurora Church, who wants to emulate the open American girl, fails to do so. She keeps striking false notes. She cannot unlearn her European training, so as to 'do very simply things that are not at all simple' (vii). Meantime, Mr Ruck suffers quizzically, as his fortune disappears in America and his wife and daughter go on spending.

The sense of impending trouble strengthens the comic grip of 'The Pension Beaurepas'. As S. G. Putt observes, the tale reveals pity for the victims of false values: 'there is a violence of disgust, of outraged compassion, lying just beneath the surface of the limpid narrative prose and light assured dialogue'.[71] The sudden departures at the close do not imply emptiness of significance. As in Shakespearian comedy (the tale has about the same number of words as *A Midsummer Night's Dream*), brevity of encounter suggests cosmic mutability. James uses the pension as a symbol of passing human phases rather than of permanent relationships. Every point is finely made, nothing overdone.

James was now poised to build a world reputation, and with *Washington Square* (*Cornhill Magazine*, June–November 1880, and *Harper's New Monthly Magazine*, July–December 1880) he began just that.

For the first time he achieved simultaneous publication on both sides of the Atlantic. Recognised at once (notably by R. H. Hutton[72]) as a work of genius, *Washington Square* revealed an intensity that was new for James. It is not only a powerful study of a woman's plight, but a sustained performance of wit, in concentrated, unfussy, American-style prose. Little longer than *The Europeans*, it is yet much denser and more economic than that, discarding atmospheric colour almost to a fault. Moving for thirty-one of its thirty-five chapters in 'very short steps' (Chapter XXXII) over a limited timespan in the 1840s, *Washington Square* deals with the wooing of Catherine Sloper, the plain daughter of a fashionable New York doctor. It lays bare every step in this process in a form of analytic drama reminiscent of Jane Austen's minutely detailed expositions of the deceptive fortunes of her heroines. The comparison with Jane Austen is often made,[73] and is justifiable, because the constant pressure of intelligently handled dialogue can be matched only in her. But the comparison is also misleading, since the plot of *Washington Square* is not underpinned by a firm social tradition. Set in a restlessly expanding city, where the way to live is to keep moving, since they 'invent everything all over again about every five years' (Chapter V), James's novel is deliberately anomalous in its foregrounding of frustration and disappointment. The ending is memorably bleak, with Catherine seating herself with her 'morsel of fancy-work', embroidering it, 'for life, as it were' (Chapter XXXV), a

Penelope for whom there has never been and never will be any Ulysses.

The contrast between the *élan* of the novelist's tone and the emptiness of his characters' lives is especially marked in *Washington Square*. Dr Sloper's keen interest is to observe whether his daughter will 'stick', and stick she does, first with her devotion to Morris Townsend and then without it; 'she is absolutely *glued*. I have passed, in consequence, into the exasperated stage' (Chapter XXVII). The comic elation in the style of the comment is undercut cruelly by the psychological devastation which is its content. Catherine's obstinate faith in her love, soon inevitably to be shattered, leaves her immobile beyond hope, with nothing to live for. The motto from Longfellow's poem of 1841, 'Excelsior', 'to keep going higher', chosen by cousin Arthur as a good one for an aspiring young couple in New York (Chapter V), is only ironically appropriate to Catherine and Morris, who end up virtually in the downcast position of the knight in the poem, lifeless with a 'hand of ice'. *Washington Square*, of course, proceeds maturely, without heroics or romantic gestures. The sensational possibilities are represented in the imagination of Aunt Penniman, whom James uses to tell the alternative melodramatic version of his story, as it were. Mrs Penniman's restlessly extravagant interpretations bring their own disappointments and some insults. Her flair was, however, unwittingly revived in Ruth and Augustus Goetz's stage and film version of 1947, known as *The Heiress*.

The key to the novel lies in Morris Townsend, who is in some ways the most conventional character – the externally glamorous figure who behaves badly, but not badly enough to attract fascination on that score. Morris Townsend's motives in seeking to marry the unattractive Catherine Sloper are never fully explained from within. Dr Sloper's unfavourable analysis of him is, however, confirmed by Mrs Montgomery's admission that he lives off her, his sister, instead of paying his way, as he claims, by tutoring her children; it is confirmed also by various inconsistencies, such as his rudeness to his supporter, Mrs Penniman. Townsend's hypocrisy emerges from occasional glimpses of his interior thoughts, for instance when he regards his future wife as a woman of 'inferior characteristics' (Chapter XV) or thinks, 'Gracious Heaven, what a dull woman!' (Chapter XXIII), when she disclaims wanting to see the sights of Europe. Townsend's desire for the easy life, his coveting the doctor's cigars, wine and well-furnished home in Washington Square, and the fact that he has wasted one fortune and is not content with the $10 000 a year that Catherine has in her own right, all tell against him. He calls off only when Catherine tells him that she has ceased to care for her father and is indifferent to the $20 000 a year remaining. Townsend's subsequent career, his marriage to a lady in Europe, who 'only flitted across his life' (Chapter XXXIV), and his failure to get himself 'thoroughly established' as a partner to a commission-merchant (though he did make himself 'comfortable', without being *caught* (Chapter XXXV)), again show him as selfish in a commonplace way without being picturesquely base. Mrs Almond, the nearest to a choric norm in *Washington Square*, may be right in guessing that Townsend, if he were to marry Catherine without the extra income, would 'hate her for his disappointment and take his revenge' pitilessly and cruelly (Chapter XXIII), but sustained passion of any sort seems unsuited to him. Catherine becomes indifferent to him only when she is awakened to his apathy: he has no incentive to stay with her beyond the financial. James admitted that Townsend was 'sketched from the outside merely and not *fouillé*',[74] but the character has a genuine menace, mediocre but resilient.

Few would agree with James's comment immediately following the one on Townsend: 'The only good thing in the story is the girl'. The doctor is outstandingly interesting, surely, and Mrs Penniman is more than a vehicle for exaggeration. There is a penetrating analysis of the way in which the childless aunt, a clergyman's widow, virtually adopts Townsend as the handsome, tyrannical son she never had. His 'very brutality came to have a sort of filial value' to her, comments the narrator with due harshness; he took his ease with her as 'he would certainly have done with his own mother' (Chapter XXVII). Mrs Penniman sentimentally substitutes Townsend's self-exhibition for the charm she believes 'would have been a natural attribute of her own progeny'. Her self-deception is unsparingly laid bare, but the passage also serves to re-emphasise the force of Townsend's extremely good looks. We already knew that 'Catherine had never seen such features – so delicate, so chiselled and finished. . . . He was tall and slim, but he looked extremely strong. . . . It seemed to Catherine

that no one who had once seen him would ever forget him'
(Chapter IV). Townsend's appearance remains the guarantee
of his insincerity. No one with such an advantage (we hear he is
'so terribly conceited') is likely to be innocent about sexual
attractiveness or to use it without an ulterior motive on one
who lacks it to the degree that Catherine does.

It is this inference which fixes Dr Sloper's opinion of
Townsend and determines his attitudes and actions, which
remain consistent to the point of self-defeat. *Washington Square* is
very much a novel about sexual feeling. Catherine is sexually
awakened (her dizziness and redness when Townsend dances
with her are the first signs) and sexually motivated, but she is
too much the Puritan American girl to be articulate about it.
The doctor sees what is happening with diagnostic clarity. He
notes that Townsend has 'quite the sort of figure that pleases
the ladies'. He tells his sister that, physically, Townsend is
'uncommonly well set up. As an anatomist, it is really a
pleasure to me to see such a beautiful structure' (Chapter VII).
Sloper's irony is of the kind that usually means two things, not
one. His devotion to science goes along with a grasp of human
psychology. He has spent 'a lifetime in study', enabling him to
classify people. Sloper has no doubt that Catherine's present
suitor neither would nor could love her. He also knows that
Catherine is too weak (by which he means her reason is
overwhelmed by her feelings) to cope with the situation. He
regards it as his duty to protect his daughter from Townsend.
James presents Sloper as eminently intelligent and perceptive;
the narrator even abstains from qualifying, near the end, the
doctor's own view that 'he had never been wrong in his life'
(Chapter XXXIII). The five-per-cent chance which he concedes
exists that he might be wrong about Townsend he eliminates in
a controlled experiment with Mrs Montgomery. The doctor
strives to maintain intellectual integrity. He had quarreled over
theology with Mr Penniman. He is genuinely interested in the
antiquities and artistic sights of Europe, as also is Townsend,
though the latter considers medicine a 'loathsome' occupation
(Chapter XVI). Sloper is not superficial or eccentric. It is
characteristic of him that, in retirement, he visits 'only those
patients in whose symptoms he recognised a certain originality'
(Chapter XXXIII). That is not to say that Sloper puts science
above people, let alone riches above people: he values science as

serving people if they will let it. He is putting into practice, indeed, the two leading American precepts, devotion to learning and devotion to practicality, which the narrator says account for the 'honour' in which the medical profession is held in America (Chapter I).

It is tempting, but wrong, to think of Sloper as avaricious and unfair. We know he married for love, not for money. Catherine's mother was a very attractive woman, who happened to be well-off. The doctor is not obsessed with wealth, though he happens to have it. His dread of vulgarity derives from a dislike of middle-class ostentation. He deplores the increase of such tastelessness, to which he sees his daughter drawn, at least in the way she dresses. 'In those days, in New York, there were still a few altar-fires flickering in the temple of Republican simplicity, and Doctor Sloper would have been glad to see his daughter present herself, with a classic grace, as a priestess of this mild faith' (Chapter III). Sloper's move up-town to 'the most delectable portion of the city' away from an area converted 'to the base uses of commerce' comes late rather than early, and can be read as a kind of rearguard action. He values his social position as appropriate to one who puts professionalism first. It blurs the issue to contend that the doctor 'is something of a fortune-hunter himself' or that he mistakes irony for urbanity, assuming it to be 'proper for his position'.[75] Sloper is made of sterner stuff than bourgeois conformism; he knows that irony is ungracious, but he warns Mrs Pennimen not to underestimate it: 'it is often of great use. It is not, however, always necessary, and I will show you how gracefully I can lay it aside' (Chapter XXVII). Sloper values irony pragmatically, because it provokes thought without offending people; it can convey a meaning indirectly, leave a hint to work its effect, amuse those who love wit. It does, however, require a degree of comprehension and good will in the auditor, and Catherine never has enough of the one and loses the other. Sloper's conservatism possibly betrays him in his low opinion of the reasonableness of women in general; but to be consistent he ought to have used other methods with Catherine. In fact, he does, but he falls back fatally on irony.

The problem dramatised in *Washington Square* is largely the difficulty of communication between one who is very clever and one who is decidedly not bright. That is why it is stylistically excellent. Catherine, though she respects her father's wisdom and is always pleased when he addresses her, unfortunately never knows what to do with his snippets of irony. Seeing them as valuable in some vague way, delicate, and contributing 'to the sum of human wisdom' (Chapter IV), she yet fails to follow their sense. Later on, she comes to deplore his irony as a poor type of expression, signifying lack of love, especially as shown in the codicil to his will (Chapter XXXIII). The narrator pinpoints Sloper's failing as 'the abuse of sarcasm in his relations with his daughter' (Chapter XXXII). The abuse is a failing, but it does follow the failure of the use. Sloper's impatience, exasperation and rather ghastly amusement at his daughter's blunders are not totally unnatural, but they are unpaternal. He admits he had to be 'quite merciless' (Chapter XXVII) in protecting her, but he has no paternal reserve of affection to fall back on, to match his sister, Mrs Almond's, 'motherly kindness to the girl', when Catherine's refusal to budge becomes final. D. W. Jefferson argues that if 'the Doctor cannot satisfy himself in one way he will do so in another', so that her resistance 'provokes him to atrocity'.[76] There is an element of truth in this judgment. Sloper's incongruous raising of his hat to Catherine in a 'stately tribute of respect' (Chapter XXX) horrifies her at the very moment she realises she has been deserted by Townsend, whose 'mask had suddenly fallen from his face'. The doctor persists, at table, in telling anecdotes about a patient's 'wonderful poodle', to which Catherine has to listen with pretended interest (Chapter XXX). These insensitive acts are possibly clumsy gestures on the doctor's part, or attempts to lighten the atmosphere and avoid direct triumph. At any rate Catherine never forgives or forgets.

Catherine Sloper's humiliation is set in the period before American girls could take up a career (James's next novel but one features a *woman*-doctor). In any case, Catherine is of the unquestioning sort, cut out to be an old-fashioned wife, 'regarding reasons as favours and windfalls' (Chapter XXIX). Her fixation upon the 'beautiful' Morris, which prevents her from marrying anyone else, is romantic, as is her reliance on will-power. James traces her development – from the plain, imperceptive, deeply feeling girl to the conservative old maid – with immense skill, contriving to preserve our sympathy for her as we are dismayed by her limitations.

This effect is achieved by the use of the indirect free style, which James learned principally from Flaubert. In giving Catherine's thoughts and summarising her attitudes from her own point of view in her own style, the narrator will obtrude the occasional phrase or passage which is clearly beyond her scope in vocabulary or expression. We know she does not like reading, she prefers Italian operas (soon to go out of date), she is proud of her copying and calligraphy, but she has never seen a foreigner and she shies away from anything clever or difficult, which she identifies with her father's studies. The modulation from echoes of her way of speaking to herself to the narrator's sophisticated constructions keeps the reader alert. Here is a short example:

> she begged him to go away, to leave her alone, to let her think. Morris went away, taking another kiss first. But Catherine's meditations had lacked a certain coherence. She felt his kisses on her lips and on her cheeks for a long time afterwards; the sensation was rather an obstacle than an aid to reflection. (Chapter X)

The allusion to Coleridge's *Aids to Reflection* clearly does not come from Catherine. The indirect free style is, however, not applied flexibly all the time in *Washington Square*. The narrator's comments may simply confirm his distance from his character, as in the analysis of Catherine's inability (an aspect of her religious inheritance) to adopt different personae towards her father and her lover:

> he could not know what she knew – how the purest love and truth were seated in the young man's eyes; but Heaven, in its time, might appoint a way of bringing him to such knowledge. Catherine expected a good deal of Heaven, and referred to the skies the initiative, as the French say, in dealing with her dilemma. She could not imagine herself imparting any kind of knowledge to her father; there was something superior even in his injustice, and absolute in his mistakes. (Chapter XVI)

Obviously, the French aphorism is quite outside Catherine's range, as is the paradoxical irony at the end. But too much sharp contrasting of register might align the reader with her father, so James uses it sparingly.

It may be the reliance on omniscient-author technique which caused James to omit *Washington Square* from the New York edition. There is the occasional platitude delivered, and there is no intelligent centre of consciousness in the story, no one in whom Catherine can confide. As it is, the narrator gives the novel its decidedly civilised tone, pointing out, for European readers, specifically American features, such as the seedier or semi-rural areas of New York, or Catherine's comparative freedom in meeting a young man. Written when James feared he was getting out of touch with American changes ('I *am* more attuned to English life now',[77] he admitted to Grace Norton after five years abroad), *Washington Square* is still unmistakeably American, not only because it vividly dramatises American cultural peculiarities, but also because of its purity of style – that democratic, educated (learnt, almost), impeccable style. We have Ezra Pound's word for it; no one, he wrote, who 'had not . . . known of some-one living in Lexington or Newton "Old Place" or somewhere of that sort in New England . . . would quite know *Washington Square* or *The Europeans* to be so autochthonous, so authentic to the conditions. They might believe the things to be "real", but they would not know how closely they corresponded to an external reality.'[78] The combination of decorous comedy and provincial limitedness is unique to James. But though the style is lucid, the interpretation of psychology and social pressures which James invites us to make is not easy. It is difficult to imagine a time when *Washington Square* will not be discussed and enjoyed.

James had long planned *The Portrait of a Lady* (*Macmillan's Magazine*, October 1880–November 1881, and *Atlantic Monthly*, November 1880–December 1881) as a major work. William James had written to him from Harvard that his recent fictional works were too slight.[79] Although at first replying that he still had 'a constant impulse to try experiments of form',[80] James, by December 1879, evidently hoped to please with the news, 'I have determined that the novel I write this next year shall be "big"'.[81] His recent popularity had strengthened his hand with his publishers. He permitted J. W. Smalley, the London correspondent of the *New York Tribune*, to inform his readers that Henry James's next production was to be 'a *serious* work

... which shall represent him at his best.'[82] The writing was done in Italy and England. The book version sold approximately fourteen thousand copies. James had reached the first peak of his career.

The Portrait of a Lady stands as James's contribution to the great nineteenth-century novel. George Eliot died during the period of its composition, and it has even been called 'a "George Eliot" novel written by James in the way he believed she *should* have written',[83] that is, presumably, without the essay-type interpolations, multiple-plot, profusion of 'characters' and painstakingly researched backgrounds which give her novels their realistic density. James's own experience was enough in itself for him to shift the scene of his heroine's crises around three countries in confidently described settings. Certainly, he retained the George Eliot conception of 'a certain young woman affronting her destiny'[84] in a world which she has yet to understand, building the episodes on the pattern of choice of marriage-partner and subsequent consciousness of mistake. Nevertheless, *The Portrait of a Lady* comes late in the series of nineteenth-century heavyweights. Compared with *Madame Bovary*, *Anna Karenina* and *Daniel Deronda*, it lacks a certain solidity. A Lady from where? the title seems to ask; framed *out of* society?

Not being based on any specific community, *The Portrait of a Lady* relies heavily on its plot. The plot chosen by James is, as Graham Greene points out, 'far from being an original one'.[85] The story of Isabel Archer's inheriting $70 000 from her uncle, who changes his will at the last moment at the secret suggestion of his consumptive son, is too good to be true; and the story of Madame Merle's persuading her former lover Osmond to marry Isabel, while concealing from her the fact that she is the mother of Osmond's daughter, is too bad to be true. Predictably, James handles this potential melodrama very circumspectly, carefully building up suspense and avoiding embarrassment (except perhaps for Madame Merle's late question, 'Have I been so vile all for nothing?' (Chapter XLIX)). Yet the absence of inevitability throws the interest away from realism. The actual acceptance of Osmond by Isabel, their wedding and early married life, are not represented, being possibly unbearable, even inconceivable. *The Portrait of a Lady* is more a symbolic individualist exploration of life than a study of social processes.

To fill out his structure, James surrounds Isabel, who is highly intelligent, attractive, good-natured and sensitive, with a small system of representative figures. The first part of the novel is devoted to Isabel's preliminary skirmishes with life: her journey to England and Italy with her aunt, Mrs Touchett, and her encounters with lovers and friends. There is little action in the novel, only the occasional visit to an art-gallery or an archaeological site, but much (too much) tea-drinking and many conversations, with Isabel either as participant or subject. The main dialogues are between Isabel and four acquaintances. There are Lord Warburton, the progressive English landowner, and Caspar Goodwood, a vigorous but stiff American businessman, both of whom court her unsuccessfully. Also there are Henrietta Stackpole, an American journalist, whose down-to-earth interpretations set Isabel's pride and idealism in relief, and Ralph Touchett, the ill cousin, a typical Jamesian observer-figure, who interferes, warns and advises from an odd position of love and impotence. In the second part of the novel, the dialogues are much tenser, featuring Isabel's husband, Osmond, and Madame Merle, as well as Pansy, their daughter, who suffers under Osmond's oppression alongside Isabel. There are also significant contributions to the debate from Mr Touchett, a retired and ailing banker of serene disposition; from Mrs Touchett, a dry, independent eccentric, who manages to be both uncommitted and decently concerned at once; from Edward Rosier, a young American art-connoisseur, who genuinely loves Pansy; and from Osmond's sister, the Countess Gemini, formerly promiscuous, but now at a loose end, who feels sorry for Isabel but strangely delays telling her that Madame Merle is Pansy's mother. The total number of significant characters scarcely exceeds this dozen; they sprawl a bit over the large canvas. They all seem rather restless or withdrawn, with gaps as they move from one location to another or emerge after intervals of time. All have attenuated family-lives, functioning either without parents or without children or without regular partners. Sometimes they seem to lack a past, though they are affected by the future and death. All but one are Americans, and all but one of *them* are expatriates. Pansy Osmond's chilling response to Madame Merle's insinuation that some day she may have a mother other than mother Catherine, 'I don't think that's necessary . . . I

had more than thirty mothers at the convent' (Chapter XXII),
is typical of so much of the tone of *The Portrait of a Lady*; mildly
witty, tentatively moral, but bleakly *deraciné*, so that the
psychological and social basis of the characters seems unstable
and unnourishing. It presents an ominous world, where
traditional values are being superseded, where fulfilment is
dependent on experiments in life rather than widespread
experience of life.[86] Of the leading characters, only Lord
Warburton, when checked, has anything to fall back upon.

In particular, in *The Portrait of a Lady*, America is not a place
to go back to. It sends out emigrants, ill-equipped for the Old
World, where they have to compromise, flounder or lie low. To
return is a kind of punishment. When Madame Merle has
finally to go back to America, which she hates, Mrs Touchett
comments:

'To America? She must have done something very bad.'
'Yes – very bad.'
'May I ask what it is?'
'She made a convenience of me.'
'Ah,' cried Mrs. Touchett, 'so she did of me! She does of
every one.'
'She'll make a convenience of America,' said Isabel, smiling
again and glad that her aunt's questions were over.
(Chapter LIV)

The understatement has a dry quality, characteristic of the
whole novel; not brilliant, but implying both ridicule and
alarm. There is a dark tinge; the shadows are of the abyss.
America lacks the qualities of a homeland. For those who have
left it, there must be a kind of hollow in the background.
America had given Isabel her ideal of independence, on which
she had prided herself. But that was hardly an upbringing. Her
father had been a feckless, indulgent spendthrift. 'The foundation
of her knowledge was really laid in the idleness of her
grandmother's house, where . . most of the other inmates were
not reading people' (Chapter III). Again we have the note of
dryness and alarm. Isabel can draw on no traditional wisdom.
The point is clear when Isabel finds Osmond so difficult a type
to classify. She is too intrigued by Madame Merle's plausible
recommendation of him:

He resembled no one she had ever seen; most of the people she knew might be divided into groups of half a dozen specimens. There were one or two exceptions to this; she could think for instance of no group that would contain her aunt Lydia. There were other people who were, relatively speaking, original – original, as one might say, by courtesy – such as Mr. Goodwood, as her cousin Ralph, as Henrietta Stackpole, as Lord Warburton, as Madame Merle. But in essentials, when one came to look at them, these individuals belonged to types which were already present to her mind. Her mind contained no class which offered a natural place to Mr. Osmond – he was a specimen apart. (Chapter XXIV)

The passage not only reveals Isabel's vulnerability (her unsuspecting assimilation of people to her own categories leaves her open to deceit); it also reveals the limits of her world, confined to a handful of new acquaintances, abstractly considered, a few representative individuals. It is the private collector's view of human relations; humanity in its national, economic, social and political relations does not impinge enough on such typifying. The absence of a familiar context for Isabel's adventure is thus integral to the novel's theme. It makes love almost impossible for her. She is a heroine who is loved, sympathises and suffers, but never falls in love. Otherwise we might have had the portrait of a woman. Unlike several other Jamesian women, Isabel Archer falls not by indulging, but by rejecting passion, which she fears may hamper her freedom of choice. She has the quality of a virginal archer, whose arrow is not directed to any earthly target.

The Portrait of a Lady is, therefore, an unconventional long-novel, but philosophically consistent. It may read in places like a comedy of manners, especially where Isabel's visitors have to be kept apart, but it is much more a novel of ideas. Its main idea, that concentration on freedom may not help one to avoid a grim servitude, stretches to the verge of tragedy. The insistence on mental liberty reminds us of German romantic idealism, which may have been what Isabel was taking in when her newly-trained mind was 'trudging over the sandy plains of a history of German Thought' just before Mrs Touchett arrived in Albany to assess her potential as a travelling-companion (Chapter III). We are told that 'Isabel was fond of metaphysics'.

The notion that individual character is free to conquer circumstances is also central to Carlyle and the American Transcendentalists. Some such influence certainly seems suggested in the scene of Isabel's 'very metaphysical' disagreement with Madame Merle. The latter lady, the perfect 'social animal' whose nature has been 'overlaid by custom', argues frankly that human beings are not isolated beings, since their selves overflow into their shells. 'By the shell I mean the whole envelope of circumstances', which includes everything that expresses and belongs to the self. Isabel counters that she knows that 'nothing else expresses me. Nothing that belongs to me is any measure of me; on the contrary, it's a limit, a barrier, and a perfectly arbitrary one' (Chapter XIX). Isabel's commitment to pure identity, admirable as it is in its disdain for materialism, is too theoretical to cope with loving people. She holds back from partnership and family life. She rejects suitors eminent in the worlds of the English establishment and American business, since both offer too narrow a sphere for her as a wife. Ralph Touchett, observing her judging life for herself, conceives the idea of putting 'wind in her sails' in order that she may gratify her imagination (Chapter XVIII). This move jeopardises her future.

The money does not alter Isabel's temperament, but it puts it in her power to bolster the aesthetic life led by Osmond. Isabel still sees herself as the 'self-sufficient American girl', who, without being fettered to a career like Henrietta Stackpole's journalism, is still in a category apart from potentially conventional wives. She prefers, vaguely, 'to think of the future than of the past' and, of all her liberties, enjoys most 'the liberty to forget' (Chapter XXI). She believes she can do fine things with her fortune, which becomes 'to her mind part of her better self'. Accepting Ralph's advice not to question her conscience so much, she attempts boldly to combine generosity with pleasure and, in her new confidence, drifts, as Henrietta had predicted, to a 'great mistake' (Chapter XVII). James shows her to be too trustful, too unrealistic, too headstrong in rejecting counsel. In Isabel Archer he associates the American traits of moral optimism and love of individual freedom with incaution in the face of evil. In an intelligent, attractive woman, the combination leads to marriage with the wrong person.

Isabel has a quality of fastidiousness which interferes with

her efforts to look deeply at life. For instance, when she pays
attention to the children, 'mainly of the poorer sort', in
Kensington Gardens, we are told her feeling of freedom throbs
into 'joyous excitement': she 'asked them their names and gave
them sixpence and, when they were pretty, she kissed them'
(Chapter XV). The singling out of pretty ones is partly an
innocent attachment to beauty on Isabel's part, but it reveals
preferences which might seriously mislead her in a crisis. Again,
in discounting Ralph Touchett's dislike of Madame Merle,
Isabel takes the delicate, but also easy, option. Ralph, having
once been in love with Madame Merle, could be expected to
sense her weak spots and he does imply she has something to
hide when he tells Isabel that the older lady's modesty is
exaggerated and 'her merits are in themselves overstrained'. Yet
Isabel still admires Madame Merle's wordly completeness
(Chapter XXIII) and desires to emulate her experienced
manner. She would rather not probe into Ralph's connection
with Madame Merle, so revealing a refinement which may be
unwise when commitments are beginning to impend. The
narrator comments, 'With all her love of knowledge Isabel had
a natural shrinking for raising curtains and looking into
unlighted corners. The love of knowledge coexisted in her mind
with a still tender love of ignorance' (Chapter XIX). Isabel's
virtuous motives transfer freedom of action from herself to her
exploiters. James's handling of his heroine's perilous career is
subtle and poignant.

Isabel is drawn to Osmond by an appreciation of his artistic
taste and an 'emotion' which involves a subdued sexual response
to his cool, still, insinuating manner. Osmond is bestirred by
the thought of marrying in a way which would enhance his own
too obscure distinction. His egotism, uninformed by anything
except envy of the powerful and luxurious, is like a base version
of Isabel's insistence on free choice. Instead of employing herself
in getting sensations, she finds herself being used to provide
them. Osmond finds her rejection of Lord Warburton especially
piquant; he 'perceived a new attraction in the idea of taking to
himself a young lady who had qualified herself to figure in his
collection of choice objects by rejecting the splendid offer of a
British aristocrat' (Chapter XXVIII). The exercise of choice
has brought Isabel to the point of being a choice object. James
explores the lesson by his choice of words, but Isabel is not to

learn it until it is too late. That she accepts Osmond in 'ardent good faith', impressed by what seems his noble uncomplaining quietness in straitened circumstances, is Ralph's view. Nevertheless James's reluctance to register Isabel's response to Osmond at the moment of acceptance (we are informed, much in the way Goodwood is, in writing, after the event) should not incline us to accept Ralph's view fully. Osmond exercises a certain physical spell upon her: she succumbs to 'a more primitive sentiment' than ardours, aspirations and theories (Chapter XXXV), secretly trembling as she assures Ralph, 'If one marries at all one touches the earth' (Chapter XXXIV). Some such half-acknowledged sexual stirring, together with her delicate incuriosity and a conviction of her own superiority of judgement to that of her advisers, is needed to account for Isabel's defiance of the signs.

The claim for *The Portrait of a Lady* to greatness rests on James's rendering of Isabel's suffering after her marriage. There can be no doubt that the last part of the novel is compelling reading. We approach Isabel some years after the wedding through the eyes of Edward Rosier, a suitor not rich enough for Pansy in Osmond's opinion, though she does reciprocate his love. Rosier, a collector of art-objects with no profession, hardly cuts a heroic figure, but his good nature serves James as a cushion to soften the bad news about Isabel. He provokes undeserved rudeness from Osmond and elicits from Madame Merle the ominous information that the Osmonds 'think very differently' (Chapter XXXVI). It is Rosier who first observes Isabel in terms of portraiture; 'framed in the gilded doorway, she struck our young man as the picture of a gracious lady' (Chapter XXXVII). Ralph Touchett sees more deeply: the grace belies the reality of pain. Isabel now has a 'charming position', but her serenity is a studied mask, to the design of which the main contributor has been, not Isabel herself, but Osmond. What Ralph notices is 'the fine lady who was supposed to represent something' (Chapter XXXIX), but the only thing she in fact represents is her husband. Isabel's desire to fly to a life at a high level of intellectual generalisation has ended with her tied to a man who constantly presents to the world a pose of mystification and impertinence.

As we enter into the inner horror of Isabel's existence, the extent of her misjudgment of Osmond is powerfully revealed.

He is felt now to have 'the evil eye', making everything wither. He hates his wife for her open, kindly way of looking at life (Chapter XLII), for having a mind of her own at all. He is intolerant and snobbish towards virtually everyone except his daughter, especially despising Henrietta Stackpole. When Isabel protests she likes to know people who are 'as different as possible' from herself, Osmond remarks, 'Why then don't you make the acquaintance of your washerwoman?' (Chapter XXXIX). His egoistic love of authority truly grinds Isabel in what Ralph calls 'the very mill of the conventional' (Chapter LIV). Osmond demands obedience in small things as well as great; he gives Isabel a list of her duties as Pansy's duenna, commands her to work for Pansy's marriage to her own old suitor, Lord Warburton ('I hold that it lies in your hands', Chapter XLI), and accuses her of intercepting a letter from Warburton to himself. It is the combination of meanness with exquisite formality that makes Osmond so odious. He always looks 'consummately uncompromised', ignoring Isabel's presence, yet recognising her 'as a disagreeable necessity of thought' (Chapter XLVI). Their disagreements heighten the tension dramatically, exemplifying that quiet, hellish scene which Isabel, fatalistically, foresees will last to the end, 'a scene of the rest of my life' (Chapter LIII).

The question why Isabel commits herself to that continuing scene dominates the reader's thoughts at the end. The narrator says nothing conclusive on the issue, but there is a lot to go on. Isabel is determined to be responsible and not escape the consequences of her deliberate act. It is partly due to her sense of decency in maintaining what was promised in her marriage-vows. There is also a deterministic element, redolent of George Eliot's idea of psychological nemesis; 'One must accept one's deeds' (Chapter XLVII). Then there is the fear of repeating her mistake; when she takes what she knows is the 'very straight path' back to her husband, after Goodwood has frightened her with his too possessive kiss (Chapter LV), the fear of a second loss of liberty is predominant, rather, I think, than a fear of sex in itself. Another factor is the restriction which Isabel feels as a nineteenth-century married woman, uncertain of alternative courses. She envies men their freedom 'to plunge into the healing waters of action', like Warburton's politics (Chapter

XXXVIII). There is also her relationship with Pansy to take into account.

It was in a feeble imitation of this Carlylean curative plunge into action that Isabel undertook to influence Pansy in favour of Warburton; it was 'some form of positive exertion. . . . To "do" – it hardly mattered what – would therefore be an escape, perhaps in some degree a remedy' (Chapter XLI). For a time she made it her duty to further her husband's wish. It is no longer in this spirit that she returns to Rome at the end. She has abandoned hope of pleasing Osmond, but she had promised Pansy to be very kind and return to her. Pansy has shown considerable courage in disobeying her father over talking to Rosier, a tenacity which Isabel comes to admire as a 'definite ideal' (Chapter L). Though when she is returned to the convent Pansy's resistance to her father collapses, she bows only negatively to his authority. Pansy is not likely to break her promise to Rosier not to marry anyone but him. Isabel has, therefore, the residual role as trustworthy confidante to Pansy. Here she displaces Madame Merle, whom Isabel, by stating her wish never to see her again, has forced away from both her daughter and Osmond. The ban can only remain in effect while Isabel is with Osmond. Another unstated motive for her return may therefore be revenge on Madame Merle (protection of Pansy amounts to that). The revenge is not damaging since Pansy already dislikes Madame Merle, as the Countess Gemini recognises when she says that Pansy has become, not Madame Merle's, but Isabel's (Chapter LI).

None of the possibilities compensates for the prospect of her living again with Osmond in 'the house of darkness, the house of dumbness, the house of suffocation'. James's imagery in conveying the agony of Isabel's married life is too powerful for anyone to suppose she can overcome her disappointment; 'she had suddenly found the infinite vista of a multiplied life to be a dark, narrow alley with a dead wall at the end' (Chapter XLII). Isabel attains the fullest recognition of her failure on the railway journey to England, undertaken against Osmond's wish, to see the dying Ralph. She sits in the corner of the compartment, with all purpose, 'all intention', suspended: 'She had gone forth in her strength; she would come back in her weakness.' The Biblical rhythm captures her essential seriousness, and points up her despair. Whenever she imagines her future self 'in the attitude of a woman who had her life to live', she reverts in turn to the prospect of enlarged suffering:

> Wasn't it much more probable that if one were fine one would suffer? It involved then perhaps an admission that one had a certain grossness; but Isabel recognised, as it passed before her eyes, the quick vague shadow of a long future. She should never escape; she should last to the end. Then the middle years wrapped her about again and the grey curtain of her indifference closed her in. (Chapter LIII)

The symbol of the long railway journey is perfectly absorbed into the meditation on life's progress in this passage. It is a measure of James's achievement in *The Portrait of a Lady* that he gives us a sense of tragedy extending into the future by keeping the central character alive.

The novel's American factor is Isabel's consciously facing her own tragedy.[87] Just as she perceives that the comical Henrietta Stackpole in marrying Mr Bantling is not surrendering her personality or renouncing her American allegiance, but is 'at last about to grapple in earnest with England' (Chapter LV), so Isabel herself, in returning to Osmond, will not surrender her personality, as happens in the convent, but will keep the 'old Protestant tradition' unfaded in her imagination (Chapter L). To do so will also be a kind of revenge on her husband, but it will be protest without independence; in other words, not the American dream, but an American nightmare.

4

Art and Conflict – 'The Aspern Papers', *The Tragic Muse*, 'The Death of the Lion'

Henrietta Stockpole's allusions to Boston radicalism and British landlordism which enliven the course of *The Portrait of a Lady* indicate the direction which James's fiction was taking in the 1880s. Three times in under a decade he matched that novel in size, but only once, the first time, in quality. Amazingly, two of these huge new works came out at the same mid-decade point; *The Bostonians* (*Century Magazine*, February 1885–February 1886) and *The Princess Casamassima* (*Atlantic Monthly*, September 1885–October 1886). *The Bostonians* is among James's masterpieces; it contains his finest writing on America and is both psychologically deep and satirically bright. *The Princess Casamassima* bravely explores the English scene in connection with revolutionary politics, a somewhat premature topic at that time, which produces in James's hands a good deal of tedium, despite the near-fascination of the ideas. This novel does, however, also touch on a theme which exercised James increasingly – the relationship between art and society. A turning-point in the story comes when the hero, the little bookbinder Hyacinth Robinson, begins to regret his commitment to take part in anarchist violence, having now grown better acquainted with the treasures of civilisation. Though becoming sceptical of the cause of redistribution of wealth, in view of 'the splendid accumulations of the happier few' (Chapter XXX), Hyacinth remains a critic of the existing social order. This character's extreme dilemma highlights the questions raised by the claims of art in an imperfect world. James now focused his own attention most acutely on the complex area of the artist's personal relationships in a period of change.

By the late 1880s the first mass-wave of beneficiaries of the 1870 Education Act had arrived on the English literary scene. The expanding market tended to cheapen literature. The foundations of the modern world and mass-culture were being laid, especially in the fields of sport, entertainment and journalism. At the same time literature was becoming more professional and institutional with literary circles organised into authors' societies, literary agencies set up, typists employed, copyright applied, university departments of English established and dead writers' homes opened to the public. The split between the highbrow and the lowbrow in the consumption of culture had set in. Into the immediately widening gap came examples of middlebrow art, like children's literature, Gilbert and Sullivan operettas and jingoistic verse. Some writers exploited the cult of personality, with public appearances and studied image more prominent than their books.

James had, of course, in the Arnoldian tradition always valued great literature as the decisive indicator of the well-being of a nation or epoch. He had pursued a celibate life of dedication to writing which not only involved commitment to the highest standards but even attempted to exemplify Arnold's ideal of the disinterested critic of life, master of at least two languages, who observed history and society from an eminence too detached for participation. Arnold had argued for culture from the secure background of an intellectual establishment with its roots in the previous century and had addressed a limited, recognisable audience sharing Classical education, Christian ethics and Romantic taste. He expected that culture to be broadened and diversified by being spread downwards by various means in the new democratic age. James settled in England in order to capture that audience, but found it diminishing. During Arnold's last years and after his death in 1888 the advent of democracy in Britain produced preoccupation with political uncertainty, agricultural depression, strikes, colonial wars, the Irish Home Rule crisis, fear of German industrial advancement and other problems. A cultural crisis was the accompaniment to this materialistic ferment. Artists turned away from the increasingly strident and commercialised features of the new mass-culture to such movements as aestheticism, impressionism and, later, modernism. Literature tended to be more esoteric, fantastic, risqué or arcane.

James, while retaining personal links with trendsetters in literature and the visual arts, was never very enthusiastic about impressionism and regarded art for art's sake as a dead end. He remained committed to the public role of the artist's work, to the employment of his imagination, that is, as he put it in his Preface to 'The Lesson of the Master', 'in the interest of morality', to the 'high and helpful public and, as it were, civic use of the imagination'. Its main role now was, he believed, to protest against 'the rule of the cheap and easy' and in this way to prevent 'the tradition of a high aesthetic temper' from helplessly perishing. At the same time, he knew that many writers lived far more in the world than he did; he recognised that imaginative impulses and curiosity about art run through all human life in various forms and that the artistic conscience is constantly being challenged and often compromised in the inextricable linkage of art and life. Here is James's subject in such tales of the literary life as 'The Private Life' (*Atlantic Monthly*, April 1892), 'Greville Fane' (*Illustrated London News*, September 1892), 'The Middle Years' (*Scribner's Magazine*, May 1893), 'The Figure in the Carpet' (*Cosmopolis*, January–February 1896) and 'The Birthplace' (*The Better Sort*, 1903). The artist in society is a multifaceted theme. The artist-figure is involved, in one way or another, in the world of money, power, sex, leisure, fashion and medicine, and his motives are rarely unmixed. In one sense, the artist, especially the novelist, is attached to this world, since it gives him his material, on which he looks 'with never-ending satisfaction',[88] but in another he is in conflict with it since it undervalues difficult art and values him for the wrong reasons. James worried sometimes lest, to avoid despair in these circumstances, he did not imagine impossibly talented artists. 'How can one consent to make a picture of the preponderant futilities and vulgarities and miseries of life without the impulse to exhibit as well from time to time, in its place, some fine example of the reaction, the opposition or the escape?'[89] He wondered whether the age could have produced writers, actors, painters, poets, editors or journalists of the quality of those he imagined. Since the age produced James himself, the difficulty of believing in his fictional artists is least when they are novelists. Generally, James succeeded very well in keeping these stories about art from being involuted or self-conscious. The main influence on them is from Browning, whose poems cover many of the same paradoxical areas of experience, where the boundary between art and life is fluid.[90] Though James avoided remote historical settings like Browning's, he was drawn to European cities for scenes where the contrast between the beautiful artistic heritage in the background and the shabby pressures of modern life in the foreground provides piquant irony.

'The Aspern Papers' (*Atlantic Monthly*, March–May 1888), one of the outstanding tales of this group, is set in Venice. This long short-story or novella contains some of the best examples of James's use of narrative suspense and atmosphere. It may be felt to be too worked-up into improbable grotesquery in parts, but the fancifulness of the first-person narrator is an inbuilt feature. 'The Aspern Papers' is certainly a very effective account of high-minded deception and double dealing among refined but isolated individuals brought together by an accident of literary history. It is based on actual events in Florence, where an American captain had taken lodgings in the house of the aged Claire Clairmont, who had once been Byron's mistress, in the hope of obtaining her literary papers. On Claire's death, these papers passed to her niece, who refused to give them to the captain unless he married her, which he declined to do. In James's tale the captain becomes an unnamed literary scholar who had been joint-editor of the poems of Jeffrey Aspern (James's imaginary American Romantic poet), Claire becomes Juliana Bordereau, daughter of an American painter who had once painted Aspern's portrait, and the niece becomes Miss Tita (Tina in the New York edition), who burns Aspern's letters in the last chapter for unexplained reasons. By shifting the scene to Venice, James is able to evoke various Gothic associations, mainly at night, suggesting a certain weirdness and moral ambiguity. A more normal perspective is provided by Mrs Prest, an older woman long resident in Venice, who is amused by her friend's infatuation with the papers and pretends 'to make light of' Aspern's genius (i), while also sounding a note of warning about Miss Tita, 'the little one'.

Dominating 'The Aspern Papers' for eight of its nine chapters, however, is the legendary Juliana, possessor of once dazzling eyes which had evoked fabulous imagery in Aspern's sonnets, now reduced to physical dependence on her niece, and obsessed both with guarding her reputation and with acquiring money. Miss Bordereau's wish not to make the letters public probably has James's endorsement (he burned correspondence he had himself received). Her willingness to turn the editor's fixed idea to profit in order to provide her niece with means is also reasonable. The narrator admits that the old lady had not always been avaricious (else she would have sold off her literary treasures years ago); 'It was I who had kindled the unholy flame; it was I who had put into her head that she had the means of making money' (vii). If she had seized his hint 'with a desperate, tremulous clutch', what else was to be expected of the aged? James gives the narrator a prose so full of comic echoes of romance, melodrama and mystery, that we are pulled two ways at once, relishing the lurid image of a cynical, cunning witch and yet harbouring offence at the insensitivity and speculativeness of the manuscript-bibber. When Miss Bordereau pronounces, 'The truth is God's, it isn't man's; we had better leave it alone. Who can judge of it – who can say?' we respect her dignity, antiquated as it may be; when the editor counters that without the support of biographical research the poet's work becomes 'vain words', with nothing by which to measure them (vii), we spot the special pleading. Yet the narrator has such a command of words himself that his account of his adventures in the old house has its own momentum of excitement. The climax comes in the scene where the old lady disturbs him just as he is about to rifle her bureau for the letters. Divested of her baffling green eye-shade behind which one could presume 'a ghastly death's head lurked' (ii), and also of the 'extemporised hood' of 'dingy lace-like muslin', she for the only time reveals her 'extraordinary eyes', glaring, and hisses out, 'Ah, you publishing scoundrel!' before collapsing in a spasm (viii). The combination of horror, farce and shame is extraordinarily good. 'I shall never forget', remarks the narrator, confident of taking us with him, 'her strange little bent white tottering figure, with its lifted head, her attitude, her expression.' At this point, as Kenneth Graham aptly says, the 'narrative flashes with the irony and fatality of their collision'.[91] No one can doubt the justice of Miss Bordereau's indignation. She had loved Aspern's letters and did not want them to be seen by prying eyes. But her other idea, the promotion of a marriage between the editor and Miss Tita, is inadmissible. The force of outrage brings on Juliana's demise and leaves the editor to negotiate, in the last chapter, with the niece.

The narrator is now required to pay the ultimate price for the papers. Miss Tita puts her proposal circumspectly; he is to join in the guardianship of the papers as a member of the family, as 'a relation' (xii). Giving no sign except embarrassment, he leaves; he is rowed, groaning softly, out into the lagoon, insisting to himself that he had not made love to her, even to get the papers. This disclaimer is strictly true. He had made it clear from early on that 'the faded facts of her person' (iii) ruled out the possibility of attraction. In any case, he is not a woman's man, unlike Aspern; he had 'not the tradition of personal conquest' (ii). Nevertheless, it is the sexual impression he makes on Miss Tita that enables him to get nearer the letters. He seems to be deceiving both her and himself. In giving her a false name for himself and a fake motive for lodging in the house, he overlooks the extent to which she may be playing him along. Trusting in her discretion and innocence, he attributes her more suspicious and pointed speeches to the influence of her aunt. But Miss Tita may confide everything to her aunt, as the latter's revelation of the Aspern portrait, so soon after the narrator's admission of interest in the poet to Miss Tita, may imply.[92] The enigma of Miss Tita's inner life is never resolved. Her final transfiguration, when her angelic look of foregiveness gives her briefly 'a sort of phantasmagoric brightness' (ix), may lead to the deduction that, on reading the letters at last, she found out that Apsern was her father, a secret which she kept by destroying the papers.[93] But it may also simply be a show of moral relief at the cessation of embarrassing complications. The episode derives its curiosity-value from the ambiguous status of the poet's letters, relevant to art but belonging to life.

So intriguing is the gap between the editor's dedication to the letters and his comprehension of their owners, that Wayne Booth singles out 'The Aspern Papers' as a prime example of double focus in fiction. Here the use of an unreliable narrator produces an 'incomplete fusion' of subject and object, of observer and observed, resulting in 'passages of mumbling', according to Booth, and 'a vague, realistic, unjudged blur'.[94] Yet we may identify with the experience of the narrator while retaining our reservations, as happens when people give us accounts of events in real life. James chooses a sufficiently sympathetic narrator – literary, stylish, morally apologetic (like some of Chaucer's narrators) – to tell a lively tale, without a guarantee of total or detailed validation. The editor clearly oversteps the mark of the permissible and deserves his ultimate discomfiture. But his mastery of the graphic, the atmospheric, the suspenseful gives his tale a power like that of 'The Ancient Mariner'. James allows him to confess without interruption his experience of hope, fear, antagonism and guesswork as he watches for his chance to acquire the prize. As Ora Segal has pointed out, the narrator, instead of recollecting, 'vividly reenacts his past adventures, with the result that the reader is hardly ever aware of the temporal gap between the distinct temporal planes of experience and narration'.[95] It is a kind of diary technique, yielding fluid drama. There is a good example when the editor moves about in the garden, wondering whether old Miss Bordereau has died: 'I looked out for Miss Tita at one of the windows, having a vague idea that she might come there to give me some sign. Would she not see the red tip of my cigar moving about in the dark and feel that I wanted eminently to know what the doctor had said?' (viii). The combination of recorded act, vivid image and guilty speculation is especially evocative and ironical, since the cigar-tip is much more likely to suggest to Miss Tita the narrator's masculinity than his anxieties over the fate of the papers. The indirection of this method seems to me more effective than any analysis of Miss Tita's actual thoughts was likely to have been.

Another point of doubt arises with regard to the letters themselves. No one questions that Byron's letters are immensely valuable papers, but, judging from the tale, would Aspern's have been? Nothing is quoted from them, nothing from the poems either, though they are said to be almost as 'divine', though not so ambiguous, as Shakespeare's sonnets (iv). James's own conventional Romantic taste in poetry rather gets in the way here. James's fear, as expressed in the Preface, lest an *American* Romantic 'adventurous lyric genius'[96] was inconceivable obfuscates the issue. The problem concerns the approach to *any* poet. What James calls the '*visitable*' past,[97] the period of Miss Bordereau's youth, is adequately recalled in the tale through the occasional image, reference or obsolete phrase. But the poet from that past seems invested with a glamorous personality which is more a matter of fantasy than historical knowledge, observation or criticism. The narrator's presumptuous worship of Aspern ('One doesn't defend one's god' (i)) seduces him into a search for traces of the dead personality. He needs, as it were, to exhume the poet. Hence he feels near to Aspern's presence when he is with Juliana, hears the voice that had been heard in Aspern's ear, sees the hand that Apsern had pressed, hatches romances about his love-life and invokes his ghost to address him intimately in the present; Aspern is fancied as saying, 'Meanwhile are we not in Venice together?' (poet and editor, that is) 'and what better place is there for the meeting of dear friends? See how it glows with the advancing summer; how the sky and the sea and the rosy air and the marble of the palaces all shimmer and melt together' (iv). If the prose of the letters is anything like this sub-Ruskinian outburst, they must be poor stuff, one feels. The air of necromantic incense is a little too thick here. James covers his tracks, however. He cannot be pinned down: the charge that James shares his narrator's uncritical stance will not stick. 'The Aspern Papers' parries all such criticism of the narrator's excess. The fact that he is left only with the Aspern portrait (the 'delightful eyes' smile 'with friendly mockery', (ix)) instead of the papers is a punishment. The portrait is an apt second-best for one who had been drawn more to Aspern's life than his poems. The pursuit of the arts is full of snares, entanglements and disappointments.

The same lesson, though in more relaxed style, is taught in *The Tragic Muse* (*Atlantic Monthly*, January 1889–May 1890), which suffers in comparison with other James stories about the arts by its spaciousness. There are two plots: one simply showing the stages of a dedicated actress's career, the other about a young man who gives up a political vocation pressed on him by his family in order to try his hand at portrait-painting. The plots are linked, rather casually, by friendships, conversations and disappointing love-affairs. The background extends with varying depth to English county politics, the classical French theatre, the diplomatic service and the aesthetic movement. Boldly, James does without Americans and writers. Long though it is, however, *The Tragic Muse* fails to satisfy because it is not long enough. Inevitably, comparisons with Trollope, Tolstoy and Conrad show up James's thinness in the world of affairs of state, and he is no match for Proust among the decadents. Using the omniscient-author technique in *The Tragic Muse*, James is inclined to be defensive and evasive as he declines to follow his characters out of view into their jobs and other essential activities. The object in focus shifts about too conveniently.

As if uneasy about this thin ice, James seems to abandon the virtue of economy in his prose in *The Tragic Muse*. The language with which he turns over problems in the characters' minds is inclined to be marred by redundancy, suggesting a beating out of matter. In passages like the following, the courteous rigmarole is too expansive:

> Certainly, to persons not deeply knowing, or at any rate not deeply curious, in relation to the young man's history, the explanation might have seemed to beg the question, consisting as it did of the simple formula that he had at last come to a crisis. Why a crisis – what was it, and why had he not come to it before? The reader shall learn these things in time, if he care enough for them. (Chapter II)

The reader's patience is likely to be tried by elaborate padding of that sort. The tendency to inflation also affects the dialogue in *The Tragic Muse*, which can be both too obvious and too desultory, even when being summed up in the narrative:

> She began to speak of this and that, and broke off to speak of something else; she talked of the theatre, of the newspapers and then of London, of the people she had met and the extraordinary things they said to her, of the parts she was going to take up, of lots of new ideas that had come to her about the art of comedy. She wanted to do comedy now – to do the comedy of London life. She was delighted to find that seeing more of the world suggested things to her; they came straight from the fact, from nature, if you could call it nature: so that she was convinced more than ever that artists ought to *live*. (Chapter XXXI)

The slackness and facility of this writing may be justified partly as an expression of Miriam Rooth's liveliness and inexperience, but there remains the impression of an author letting himself go on about very little.

On the other hand, *The Tragic Muse* does contain many serious arguments, long and short, about art, such as Gabriel Nash's speech about artists' duty to recognise the particular form that suits them and to master their instruments: 'Those fine processes in themselves classify us' (Chapter XXIII). Miriam Rooth's admirer, the diplomatist Peter Sherringham, is another who is given challenging insights. He sees that the actress is no mere mimic, but an intuitive experimenter: 'Miriam's performance was a living thing, with a power to change, to grow, to develop, to beget new forms of the same life' (Chapter XXXI). Such ideas seem almost Coleridgean, but because so much of the novel is about artists' finding their feet, the discursive element is somewhat provisional and unresolved. Many of the leading characters in *The Tragic Muse* are presented as erratic and inconsistent, which is quite forgiveable, but does not make for overall coherence. It might have been better had James used the omniscient-author convention to develop such points more precisely, since the author's commitment to his art is evidently less compromised than that of his characters. But James would not revert to such an out-of-date manner.

J. I. M. Stewart is broadly right, I think, in his verdict that *The Tragic Muse* is in the end a 'strangely inert novel'.[98] The theme of dissatisfaction with the new age underlies much of its animated surface. The artist-figures seem in the end to be going nowhere very fast. Miriam Rooth has the most talent, honesty, determination and public success, yet even she is frustrated by the conditions of the commercial theatre of the day, such as the tyranny of the 'long run', and is not properly appreciated by 'the great childish audience' (Chapter LI). She emulates the French star, Mlle Voisin, who puts more into being a 'celebrity' than did the older, classic, more 'academic' actress, Mme Carré (Chapters XX and XXI). Miriam marries the shallow Basil Dashwood, an actor-manager, for convenience, not love, and admits, 'I think I'm disgusting, with my successful crudities. It's discouraging; it makes one not care much what happens. What's the use, in such an age, of being good?' (Chapter XLVIII). The note of uncertainty extends to Nick Dormer, who, sacrificing his seat in the House of Commons and his prospective marriage to a woman of political influence, the widowed Julia Dallow, Sherringham's sister, makes no special contribution to painting, leaves at least three portraits unfinished and ends up painting for 'Society', with marriage to Mrs Dallow not ruled out after all. His sister Biddy apparently thinks no more of her ambition to be a sculptress when she gets the chance to marry Peter Sherringham, once it is settled that Miriam Rooth will not give up the stage for the same purpose. Again, the representative aesthete and lover of paradoxes, Gabriel Nash, though he encourages others to take up art, seems to lose interest in them once they have done so. Nash seems to have no contacts outside the main figures in the novel, refuses to sit on till his portrait is finished and disappears without a trace, 'like a personage in a fairy-tale or a melodrama' (Chapter XLIX). A curious amalgam of Wilde, Pater, and certain dilettante figures known to James, Nash gives the impression of being too bowdlerised to bear scrutiny. In fact, all the characters in *The Tragic Muse* hold themselves carefully aloof from Bohemianism.

On the other hand, James does get across the physical impact of his two main contrasted women in *The Tragic Muse*. The two young men involved, Peter Sherringham and Nick Dormer, are perhaps too alike in their scrupulous restraint and long-winded indecision. But, particularly in Sherringham's case, there are some subtle explorations of self-deception and genuine impulse. He is shown as definitely under the spell of the girl for whose training on the stage he had, as a lover of the theatre, privately paid. He gives Miriam Rooth the benefit of tuition from the veteran of the *Comédie Français*, Madame Carré, at the same time being dismayed that there is no equivalent national theatre in England for her to aspire to join. Sherringham is given his share of prejudice, as he finds himself trying to undo his own work and persuade Miriam to leave the stage to marry him: 'he was conscious, in his person, of a cessation of resistance which identified itself absurdly with liberation' (Chapter XLV). There is irony, and even some pathos, in the way that, as a rejected suitor, he keeps on proposing and in his frustration is reduced to a Philistinism similar to his sister's. Miriam, the 'objective' centre of the novel,[99] is too much the studied personality to be 'done' from the side, but her painful feelings emerge too in the dialogue.

The younger characters' conversation causes James some

difficulties in _The Tragic Muse_. He makes heavy weather of the English way of speaking. A few phrases like 'Upon my word', 'Bless my soul', 'By Jove' and 'I say – I say –I say' are made to do a lot of work, and others like 'There's the rub', 'Verily, verily' or 'In the name of all the Muses' are embarrassingly laboured.

James does, however, prove to have an ear for English idiom in his satire on parliamentary politics in _The Tragic Muse_. Admittedly, the gaps in this side of the novel – the absence of vote-counting, lobbying, particular bills, issues or point-making – is very obvious.[100] James, no doubt, felt he had demonstrated enough concern for social causes in _The Princess Casamassima_, and now was attempting a more oblique approach. Lady Agnes Dormer and Mrs Dallow are deliberately shown as taking too elevated and inarticulate a line on public duty for the details of political issues to matter to them. That is their weakness; with no political career open to them, they have to rely on inspiring their menfolk. Through them, James acutely exploits the English fondness for understatement and superior slang to mock the institution of Parliament, which has more prestige than is good for it and takes its incomparability too much for granted. Nash's wry reference to it as 'your own theatre' (Chapter XXIV) is partly justified. There are some highly comic misunderstandings here, the basis of which is both linguistic and moral. Such phrases as 'bringing him in for Harsh' or 'putting him in the House' refer to Julia Dallow's exertions as a great landed proprietor to pull the voters round behind Nick Dormer, but they have curious undertones not evident to the users. So, Julia's 'man' means the 'fellow that stands', stands for Parliament that is (Chapter III). Julia's companion's exclamation, 'It's a wonderful constitution', provides another joke, Nick being on the point of saying 'The British? Wonderful!' when he perceives she is praising Julia's 'fine robustness' (Chapter XIV). Julia has a Betjemanesque physicality, which Nick evidently likes. There is a very amusing episode in the proposal scene, in which Julia happens to be carrying Mr Hoppus's essay on the revision of the British constitution, 'the article of the month', as she designates it to Nick. They leave it behind by mistake in the pavilion on an island in Julia's lake, that 'liberal sheet of water', but she reassures Nick;

'It doesn't signify. I have another one at home.'

'Another summer-house?' suggested Nick.

'A copy of Mr. Hoppus.'

'Mercy, how you go in for him! Fancy having two!'

'He sent me the number of the magazine; and the other is the one that comes every month.'

'Every month – I see', said Nick, in a manner justifying considerably Mrs. Dallow's charge of vagueness. They had reached the stile and he leaned over it, looking at a great mild meadow and at the browsing beasts in the distance.

'Did you suppose they come every day?' asked Mrs. Dallow.

'Dear no, thank God!' They remained there a little; he continued to look at the animals and before long he added: 'Delightful English pastoral scene. Why do they say it won't paint?'

'Who says it won't?'

'I don't know – some of them. It will in France; but somehow it won't here.'

'What are you talking about?' Mrs. Dallow demanded.

Nick appeared unable to satisfy her on this point. (Chapter XV)

Julia is as vague about the problem he raises as he is about the need to reform the British constitution. Temperamental similarities underlie the divergence of their interests. The incongruities lie lightly on a nexus of interrelated merits and demerits in their characters and in English culture, well understood by James.

The best things in *The Tragic Muse* come in Nick's visits to Mr Carteret, his ailing patron, at Beauclere. A Whig grandee who had been active in the politics of the 1840s, but never made it to the top or, indeed, married, Carteret encourages Nick with blinkered benevolence. James comments directly on Carteret's antique political vocabulary, 'untainted' by modern American usage; it emerges as being at once colourful and deadening (Chapter XVI). The story of the withdrawal of Carteret's promise of a huge legacy for Nick as he learns how little Nick is committed to his responsibilities as an M.P., how he is not to marry Mrs Dallow after all and how, finally, he is to resign his seat and take up art, is managed with great finesse. The whole Beauclere household, with its heavy furniture, impeccable, blank butler, 'orderly debate' at dinner, and timid sister, Mrs London, who decently abstains from taking advantage of Nick's disappointing attitude, is most convincingly realised. The climax comes when the old man, misinterpreting Nick's reference to 'very small souls' in his own party, bursts out, 'God forgive you, are you a Tory – are you a Tory?' (Chapter XXXIII), probably the funniest moment in all James. Carteret cannot accept that the noble life is to do one's work well, whatever it may be, a point where Nick Dormer is closer to George Eliot than to the *fin de siècle* generation. The delicate treatment of the old is a feature of *The Tragic Muse*; Madame Carré is sketched with as much awareness as is Mr Carteret, and with more affection. The mothers in the story, Nick's and Miriam's, are equally deftly handled; their characters, despite the differences in their experience of society, seem to converge due to apprehension for the future. James seems happier with the past than the present in *The Tragic Muse*, a novel where the imaginative pressure is intermittent and confidence wavers. He needed a more economical form to make his points about art effectively. Lily Briscoe in Virginia Woolf's *To the Lighthouse* (1927), which, no doubt, was written from a more advantageous point in time, shows better than Nick Dormer the way the living, working artist has to be done in the novel.

A good example of a more limited and polished performance in this field is 'The Death of the Lion' (*The Yellow Book*, April 1894), where James is back on the firmer ground of the world of books. The first of three tales of literary life contributed by James to Henry Harland's new quarterly (the others were 'The Coxon Fund', July 1894, and 'The Next Time', July 1895), it shows that James was in full command of the short novel form during the period he was writing plays. He was given by Harland all the space he wanted, to express, 'elegantly', any idea he might wish, 'an offered licence that, on the spot, opened up the millenium to the "short story"',[101] as James acknowledged appreciatively. He used this freedom primarily to concentrate his resources, however. 'The Death of the Lion' is as crowded and succinct a piece as James ever wrote.

Planned to correspond to 'a reality that strikes me every day of my life', 'The Death of the Lion' sustains itself buoyantly, remaining as 'admirably satiric, ironic' as James intended. The 'reality' is the absence of a genuine habit of reading literature among those who crowd in on the literary world, fête authors socially or write popular articles about them. At the same time the tale presents a sympathetic portrait of a literary enthusiast in the person of the journalist-narrator, 'my critical *reflector* of the whole thing, a young intending interviewer who has repented, come to consciousness, fallen away',[102] defected, that is, from the gossip-column ethos. So the gallery of sycophants lionising the refined novelist, Neil Paraday, is viewed aghast by his true critic, who also converts a visiting American autograph-hunter, Miss Fanny Hurter, to the belief in the need for abstinence from personal contact with the author. Certainly James is very favourably placed in 'The Death of the Lion' for exhibiting his strengths. The narrator is a more sensitive, unselfish version of the editor-*raconteur* in 'The Aspern Papers'. The charming American girl is a more positive representative of the idealistic side of American culture than earlier James heroines. She soon adapts to the situation, makes it a point of honour to put Paraday's works before the man, and joins the narrator at the end both in marriage and in the search for the lost Paraday scenario. Here is a wholly clean literary quest.

'The Death of the Lion' also avoids problems of specificity with regard to the central artist-figure. Paraday's talent is implicit in the texture of the tale, in which the evocative, witty prose is attributed to his disciple. James admitted that the material for such tales about writers who have to pay for their sincerity was 'drawn preponderantly from the depths of the designer's own mind'.[103] Though Paraday has non-Jamesian appurtenances like a separated wife and recurrent heart-disease, nevertheless, his difficult style of novel, choice of country retreat, fondness for youthful acolytes and tendency to make the preliminary sketch so rich that it supersedes the product itself are all prophetic glimpses of the way James's subsequent achievement and decline were to go. In fact, the scene in the 'little provincial home' in which the refined journalist discusses with the 'dear master' the difficulties of turning 'the written scheme . . . the overflow into talk of an artist's amorous plan' into a novel when it was already 'really, in summarised splendour, a mine of gold, a precious, independent work' (iii) anticipates later events so uncannily as to suggest that, for James, life deliberately imitated art – his own art. On the other

hand, Paraday surrenders to the temptation of publicity so
weakly that the tale is also cautionary. Paraday had hoped to
use the narrator as an 'encircling medium' to protect him from
interference while the next great task is completed, but he
succumbs to the press in spite of himself, almost to his own
surprise. An unexpected puff in a third leader in *The Empire*, the
'big blundering newspaper', leads to a round of engagements in
the London 'season', photographs, sittings for a hack portraitist,
Mr Rumble, meetings with royalty and visits to country-houses
which finish him off. James has a field-day here, producing a
dozen or more sharply delineated figures ranging from the
Home Counties to California to prey upon his novelist with
more or less conscious persistence.

There may be a query why Paraday collaborates so weakly;
he makes hardly any use of the narrator's service as minder.
Inured to obscurity for so long, Paraday is afraid of his new
patrons, especially of Mrs Weeks Wimbush, the wife of a
wealthy brewer, who collects all the latest celebrities for her
weekends at Prestidge. There is, however, no close feminine
companion, as there is in 'The Author of "Beltraffio"' (*English
Illustrated Magazine*, June–July 1884) or 'The Lesson of the
Master' (*Universal Review*, July–August 1888), to divert his
loyalty from his art. Mrs Wimbush is merely using Paraday's
name; the narrator calls her 'a blind, violent force, to which I
could attach no more idea of responsibility than to the creaking
of a sign in the wind' (vi). But so keen is Paraday's imaginative
feel for others' feelings, appetites and motives that he could no
more disappoint Mrs Wimbush than he could 'overturn that
piece of priceless Sèvres' (ix). It was partly with the object of
studying such human material that Paraday had consented to
join the social circus. 'The Death of the Lion' is, then, among
other things an exemplification of the paradox that writers'
material may be dangerous to their survival.

On another level it explores a conflict between what Suzanne
Kappeler calls the literary community and the context of
society. In the literary community, she says, the initiated literati
understand 'that the author ought to be a literary subject who
had best remain socially anonymous', yet they have to fight in
the social context for his success in terms of the 'distribution of
his product'.[104] Fame and money draw him into a social sphere
where his work is actually little appreciated and the work of

inferior authors much preferred. It is this perception which accounts for the narrator's righteous anger and even bitterness. The casualness with which Paraday is allowed to die at Prestidge, and the precious scenario to be mislaid, is a consequence of confused values. This theme is present from the start, where the narrator's new boss is said to have 'accepted the high mission of bringing the paper up', following the 'lowering system' to which its previous owner had subjected it (i). The improvement is superficial, however, since 'up' signifies only 'up-market', and the narrator's new mission is only to write Neil Paraday 'up', where to 'write up' means to contribute an essay on his personality. The narrator writes a critical essay on the novels instead, and leaves his job. An emissary of the new journalism is Mr Morrow, representing an international syndicate of thirty-seven influential journals, who also writes a gossip-column. Morrow champions popular writers who, often using transsexual pseudonyms, practise 'the larger latitude', that is, greater sexual explicitness. One such bestseller, 'Guy Walsingham', in fact Miss Collop, actually recites from her own work at Prestidge, when another, the weird 'Dora Forbes' arrives.

> Dora Forbes lifted his bushy brows. "Miss Collop?"
> "Guy Walsingham, your distinguished *confrère* – or shall I say your formidable rival?"
> "Oh! growled Dora Forbes. Then he added: "Shall I spoil it if I go in?"
> "I should think nothing could spoil it!" I ambiguously laughed. (x)

The farce arising here from getting lost 'among the genders and pronouns' (ix) symbolises the instability of taste that prevails in the consumer-markets for fiction. 'The Death of the Lion' is unquestionably one of James's most sharply focused, enjoyably written and amazingly clairvoyant stories, full of humane touches and pointed caricature. It emphasises what was James's own opinion on these matters, that literary and artistic achievement is rare and hard-won, that there is a duty to identify it, rescue it and preserve it and that the great writer's effort and courage are matched only by those of his critic.

5

English Morality – *The Spoils of Poynton, What Maisie Knew,* 'The Turn of the Screw'

When James, after the failure of *Guy Domville* in 1895, withdrew from his attempt to conquer the London stage, he felt he had been brought face to face with some very ugly aspects of English life. The audience, for example, had made more of a spectacle of itself than the cast. The popular element in the theatre had, with 'malice prepense', openly sided with the villain of the piece, Lord Devenish, and had failed to appreciate Guy, the last of the Domvilles, James's renunciatory hero. When he took his author's curtain-call, James found himself at the centre of a storm of derision and applause which was more than just critical, but moral. 'All the forces of civilization in the house', he wrote to his brother, 'waged a battle of the most gallant, prolonged and sustained applause with the hoots and jeers and catcalls of the roughs, whose *roars* (like those of a cage of beasts at some infernal "zoo") were only exacerbated (as it were!) by the conflict.'[105]

Returning, inwardly bruised and battered, to the production of novels, James turned his attention to subjects more heavily laden with evil, where goodness seems frail and vulnerable, than those used in his earlier, expansive works. He concentrated for the next six years or so on more concise stories, featuring various kinds of moral outrage among English people. Theft, deception, treachery, divorce, psychological vampirism, hardness of one sort and another contribute a grimness to these works. A prominent preoccupation is the neglect, abuse, spoiling, even corrupting of young people and children. The relaxed and sometimes weary wit of the novels concerning art gives way to a tenser prose, probing for unexplained horror and atrocity. The sorrow and alarm contained in such works often approach hysteria and despair. It is as though James's moral equilibrium has been jolted during this *fin de siècle* period.

At the same time, any feeling of panic engendered by this apprehension of a moral abyss was to be checked and controlled by a careful application of 'technique' to the presentation of the subject. In this connection, James began to consider ways of turning his experience as a playwright to advantage. He planned the new novels very studiously, working from detailed scenarios as with plays. He said that the scenario has a '*singular value for a narrative plan too*', giving him 'from point to point, each of my steps, stages, tints, shades, every main joint and hinge, in its place, of my subject'. The plans were quite freely altered in various particulars as he went along. But there is no doubt that James's fiction after 1895 gives the impression of pervasive authorial control, with every phrase and incident making a contribution to the whole, with nothing irrelevant or redundant. From his theatrical experiments James had, he believed, gained a certain 'mastery of fundamental statement – of the art and secret of it, of expression, of the sacred mystery of structure'.[106] James became much more selective over details. Artistic economy came first. Decisive moves in the plot were now often reported indirectly or discussed retrospectively in 'scenes' featuring peripheral characters; or they might be divined during meditations by especially perceptive observers impressed by some significant details of the 'picture', whether of a room, building or landscape. Both methods, picture and scene, impression and dialogue, are held to be dramatic because they are set up by the author as objective examples of experience for the reader to appreciate. James dramatises his characters, not only by their gestures and speech, but also by their consciousness. The development of his situation becomes inward as his most sensitive protagonists try to resolve their uncertainties. The dialogues too become increasingly elusive and obscure, as the interlocutors guess thoughts, avoid the obvious, base congratulations on unstated understandings and bandy words belonging to private codes. In certain novels, especially *The Awkward Age* (*Harper's Weekly*, October 1898–January 1899) and to a lesser extent *The Sacred Fount* (1901), dialogue predominates; in others, long paragraphs of reflections are interrupted by only a single remark, the ramifications of which may require pages of analysis before the reply can be noted. James felt the attractions of both tendencies. Thus we find him reminding himself in his *Notebooks* at one point that 'the *scenic* [*i.e.* dialogue] method is my absolute, my imperative, my *only* salvation' and at another point that there 'can be almost no dialogue at all. This is an iron law. It is absolute.'[107]

Actually, novels so deeply pondered and cherished in the unwinding as these later ones of Henry James look in the end very unlike plays. They lack the dramatic effects of surprise and quickness. It is the objectivity of drama, especially Shakespearean drama, that James was after. His shyness *vis-à-vis* his audience and his conviction of the unspeakableness of much of life, its hidden seeds of disaster, led him to abandon the role of raconteur and literary personality, the novelist within the novel, and to let the fictional situations speak for themselves, with the characters offering rival but not definitive interpretations. This impersonality amounts in a way to dramatisation.

The withdrawal of James the author from his narratives works best when he is sure of his subjects and at least their main probable effects. In those cases, uncertainty in the characters, whether as regards their knowledge or their assessment of what is happening, is a gain in irony. But any latent uncertainty in the subjects themselves can compound the problems of interpretation of these novels to a dizzying degree. The first important example of James's later type of novel, *The Spoils of Poynton* (first published as 'The Old Things', *Atlantic Monthly*, April–October 1896), contains such an internal shift of emphasis. We can observe here the transition from a preoccupation with art to a concentration on painful issues of behaviour, the word 'spoils' in the title denoting stolen goods rather than objects of beauty. James's idea for *The Spoils of Poynton* derived from an anecdote which he had heard from a Mrs Anstruther-Thompson about a young Scottish landowner who had returned home with his bride upon his father's death in order to take over the family house and its valuable contents, 'pictures, old china, etc., etc.',[108] only to find that his mother had already removed them. James was at first interested in the mother's view of the situation. In his (English) version of the story Mrs Gereth is an art-collector of outstanding taste who has transformed her Jacobean home, Poynton, into a complete work of art. Unfortunately, her son Owen, attracted and soon engaged to Mona Brigstock, a strong-willed, acquisitive girl from a Philistine background, is indecisive and vague in an upper-class way. The first theme in the novel, the mother's desperate single-mindedness in preserving her life's work from the abuse she is certain it would suffer at the hands of someone like Mona, is handled by James with assurance and panache. The opening scene, in which Mrs Gereth endures the aesthetic misery of the Brigstocks' ugly home, is one of his most promising:

> It was hard for her to believe that a woman would look presentable who had been kept awake for hours by the wallpaper in her room; . . . she was, as usual, the only person in the house incapable of wearing in her preparation the horrible stamp of the same exceptional smartness that would be conspicuous in a grocer's wife. She would rather have perished than have looked *endimanchée*. (Chapter I)

The extravagant tone captures the conscious superiority of taste exactly, while also initimating the uncompromisingness, not quite amounting to ruthlessness, which will soon land Mrs Gereth in trouble. James believed, however, that such a character's consciousness lacked the intensity and flexibility to do more than introduce the novel. Before the end of the chapter he switches the point of view permanently to Fleda Vetch, a middle-class girl, undistinguished in appearance, who shares Mrs Gereth's artistic standards and becomes her companion.

As the plot unfolds, the emphasis, though not to the same extent the interest, in *The Spoils of Poynton* is transferred away from the Gereths' quarrel over the treasures to its emotional repercussions upon Fleda. Mrs Gereth schemes to use Fleda, who is ultra-scrupulous and diffident, to distract Owen from his engagement to Mona Brigstock. If only he would marry Fleda instead, Mrs Gereth perceives, the art-collection would have its ideal custodian. Fleda, however, is aware that manoeuvrings which succeeded during the acquisition of the objects are much less suited to the manipulation of personalities. The passages in which Fleda responds with a mixture of admiration and disapproval to Mrs Gereth's audacity in first removing and

then returning the things to Poynton maintain the critical poise
of the opening of the novel:

> And what most kept her breathless was her companion's very
> grandeur. Fleda distinguished as never before the purity of
> such a passion; it made Mrs Gereth august and almost
> sublime. It was absolutely unselfish – she cared nothing for
> mere possession. She thought solely and incorruptibly of
> what was best for the things; she had surrendered them to
> the presumptive care of the one person of her acquaintance
> who felt about them as she felt herself, and whose long lease
> of the future would be the nearest approach that could be
> compassed to committing them to a museum. (Chapter
> XVIII)

Fleda's omission of the complicating human emotions
surrounding the 'one person' mentioned, namely herself, gives
this account of her companion's extraordinary character a
powerful irony.

Nevertheless, those emotions increasingly dominate the novel,
leading to the disappointment which makes 'the cup overflow',
when Fleda's tears get 'beyond control' and Mrs Gereth, too,
'soundlessly, wearily wept' (Chapter XX). James conceived of
Fleda in two ways, first as one of his 'registers or "reflectors"'
in whom lives 'appreciation, even to that of the very whole',
and second as a fallible participant in a love story, one who is
not 'distinctively able', because, 'obliged to neglect inches, [she]
sees and feels but in acres and expanses and blue perspectives'.[109]
Fleda wastes her one great opportunity of passion because of
her heroic fineness of conscience. James complicates his story of
the spoils by concentrating on Fleda's selfless love for the
eminently masculine but rather bewildered Owen and on his
tentative response to her. Instead of rescuing him from Mona,
for whom he feels, he says, less and less, Fleda holds back
scrupulously from admitting her feelings. Mrs Gereth having
restored the spoils to Poynton prematurely, in order to put
pressure on Fleda to 'let herself go' with Owen, Fleda, quite
unrealistically, requires Mona 'in black and white, as you may say',
to give Owen his freedom first (Chapter XVIII). Since Mona had
made the return of the spoils a condition of continuing the
engagement, she is hardly likely to give Owen up now. In this

way Fleda is doomed by her own conscientiousness to lose
Owen, and the spoils too are doomed, since Mona, in the event,
leaves them in charge of incompetent caretakers, to be destroyed
in a fire. Such is Fleda's idealism that she wants Owen to come
to her unsullied. 'You'll be happy if you're perfect', she
sententiously warns him, admitting to herself that for that
reason he never could be happy (Chapter XVI). Fleda believes
that it should not be Owen who breaks the engagement: he
must never be cruel to Mona; nothing should be said against
him. Fleda's altruism puts an engagement virtually on the same
plane as a marriage. She remains unsure of Owen's love for
herself, as she explains, but she removes the means by which
she could be sure.

In *The Spoils of Poynton* James had not yet developed the use
of *ficelle*-characters, those who convey to the reader essential
information which the central character either does not know or
does not care to explain. The reader, therefore, never knows
what the exact state of the relation between Mona and Owen
is, how far he is torn between her and Fleda and whether Fleda
is assuming too much. James's prose reaches a new pitch of
subtlety and elusiveness as Fleda imagines what game the
engaged two are playing at Waterbath, Mona's family home,
where Mona is passively nursing a resentment against Fleda
and Mrs Gereth for their intervention. Hearing nothing from
Owen, Fleda feels stupefied:

> Fleda had no real light, but she felt that to account for the
> absence of any result of their last meeting would take a
> supposition of the full sacrifice to charity that she had held
> up before him. If he had gone to Waterbath it had been
> simply because he had to go. She had as good as told him
> that he would have to go; that this was the inevitable incident
> of his keeping perfect faith – faith so literal that the smallest
> subterfuge would always be a reproach to him. When she
> tried to remember that it was for herself he was taking his
> risk, she felt how weak a way that was of expressing Mona's
> supremacy. There would be no need of keeping him up if
> there were nothing to keep him up to. Her eyes grew wan as
> she discerned in the impenetrable air that Mona's thick
> outline never wavered an inch. She wondered fitfully what
> Mrs Gereth had by this time made of it, and reflected with a

strange elation that the sand on which the mistress of Ricks had built a momentary triumph was quaking beneath the surface. (Chapter XVII)

Fleda's perfectionism works so much against her own interest that it is hard not to be impatient with James for not distancing himself from her. Even the phrase 'strange elation' is to be construed as appreciative, and the mention of wanness in the eyes suggests a bid for sympathy. James wanted this 'sacrificial exaltation'[110] of Fleda's, the essence of *The Spoils of Poynton*, to come across dramatically, even though it is a less fierce emotion than sexual passion. But there is a hovering sense of misjudgment about Fleda's moral heroism which leaves one uncomfortable. She is not presented as faultless, being inclined to romanticise her experience of men and to indulge in tactless remarks to or contemptuous thoughts about those whom she considers her inferiors. Commentators have had all sorts of responses to Fleda Vetch, from warm approval to sharp denigration,[111] and this instability in critical reaction is not accidental. Unlike other Jamesian girl-figures, such as the unnamed telegraphist of *In the Cage* (1898), who have relationships to loyal, ordinary characters like Mr Mudge, Fleda seems too perilously anchorless to be entrusted with the point of view. She does not make the obvious mistakes of Strether in *The Ambassadors* (1903), the novel which *The Spoils of Poynton* most resembles in technique, without approaching its comic tone. The painful elaboration of Fleda's exalted dilemma lacks true poignancy.[112] Had she been an American girl, we would have been surer how to take her. There is, in fact, a welcome touch of independence at the end, when with 'the raw bitterness of a hope that she might never again in life have to give up so much at such short notice' (Chapter XXII), she quickly returns to London.

What Maisie Knew (*Chap-Book*, January–August 1897), by way of contrast, concentrates on a single theme, the development of a child of divorced parents. Its objectivity is gained, however, at the expense of a certain loss of fluency. It is one of those novels which grow longer as the end is neared. After a brisk start, it slows down about two-thirds of the way through. There is some appropriateness in this retardation, as it corresponds to the complications of approaching maturity in Maisie. But it is characteristic of all later James stories that the development takes him many more words to work out than he had expected. Economy of narrative technique goes with a generous expressiveness in the style. As the tail of *What Maisie Knew* uncoils itself in the sometimes dragging Boulogne scenes (Chapters XXII to XXXI), signs of oral composition can be detected. It is known that James abandoned writing for dictating to a typist while doing *What Maisie Knew*. Chapter XX is as likely a place to mark the change as any, when effects appear like Sir Claude's holding his watch long enough to give Maisie 'a vision of something like the ecstacy of neglecting such an opportunity to show impatience'. Here the abstraction and negation seem to spring from the exploratory speaking voice of Henry James rather than belong to the finished written sentence. The eye rejects the bunches of sounding phrases. At the start of *What Maisie Knew*, when the Faranges' divorce is being anatomised, the language is witty and trenchant; the patterns are those of prose on paper. 'Their rupture had resounded, and after being perfectly insignificant together they would be decidedly striking apart' (Introduction). A sentence like that could not occur at the end of the novel, where unpunctuated parentheses and intrusive qualifications spin out the prose to a density which makes few concessions to immediacy of impact. As Maisie, for instance, gropes for an explanation of Sir Claude's behaviour, the narrator comments: 'She had ever of course in her mind fewer names than conceptions, but it was only with this drawback that she now made out her companion's absences to have had for their ground that he was the lover of her stepmother' (Chapter XX). Every word is weighed and cherished; the reader scans in vain for a quick signification from what is, in effect, the record of a studied utterance. Of course, the sheer punctilio with which the narrator steps from his own to Maisie's point of view, then through hers into that of the others, and back, in these passages is fascinatingly artful. Not a shade of contrast between the psychological and the colloquial, the evasive and the abusive, is lost. The irony extends to the oddest details of the child's and the adults' worlds, as Maisie progresses in the harsh school of life from knowing virtually nothing to being 'distinctly on the road to know Everything' (Chapter XXVI)). The later style can suggest

an almost seamless continuity, which is suitable for conveying a
process of maturation, whose stages, unmarked by dates and
age, merge one into another.

Maisie rejects in the end all her relatives, her parents Ida
and Beale, her step-parents, Mrs Beale and Sir Claude, and all
their other connections, in favour of her dowdy and not
especially intelligent governess, Mrs Wix. She plumps for the
one person who unreservedly loves her. Maisie has learned to
value affection above attraction, caring above style, good-
heartedness above social and sexual distinction, and settles for
a credible future with a possibility of happiness. Even so, it is
made clear that Maisie would have preferred the protection of
Sir Claude to that of Mrs Wix, if only he had passed her test of
giving her first priority. Sir Claude's generosity and *savoir-faire*
as a ladies' man strongly appeal to Maisie; she is more in tune
with his tolerant view of personal relations than with Mrs
Wix's moral censoriousness. Sir Claude is weakly afraid of Mrs
Beale, however, and can never give her up. Maisie knows from
of old that her stepmother does not really care for her, so she
has no alternative but to stick with Mrs Wix, personally gross
and educationally unrefined as she may be, for the last stage of
her journey to adulthood.

We should not be too disturbed by Maisie's selfish stirrings
before she decides upon respectability. She has had to look after
herself from the early days of imposed insecurity, when 'the idea
of an inner self or, in other words, of concealment' rose in her
as a new remedy for 'the feeling of danger' (Chapter II). The
wonder is that Maisie consistently deals with others so justly.
Maisie makes two offers to Sir Claude near the end: first to
accompany him by train to Paris, on the way to realising her
vision of 'the stepfather and the pupil established in a little
place in the South while the governess and the stepmother, in a
little place in the North, remained linked by a community of
blankness', and second, no doubt with the same improbable
solution in view, to wait for him on the Boulogne rampart, 'on
that old bench where you see the gold Virgin' (Chapter XXXI),
both times without even having said goodbye to Mrs Wix. Both
propositions may seem to involve harsh treatment of the
governess, but Maisie knows that Mrs Wix's opposition to
them as they stood would have been total and also that Mrs
Wix would have been an awkward third member of the party

with Sir Claude, whom she had just embarrassed with a too affectionate offer to serve him. So Maisie's willingness to sacrifice Mrs Wix in the interest of her supreme good, a life with Sir Claude, is excusable. That this supreme good of Maisie's imagination, however, includes offering herself physically to Sir Claude in under-age sex as a bribe is surely an unwarranted gloss. She thinks of herself as his adoring pupil. That she could be capable of crude corruption herself, having seen so clearly what it is in others, contradicts the gravamen of the whole novel.[113]

Not that James by any means excludes the idea of the girl's incipient sexuality. Maisie has not accepted that it is a crime for two people to live together in love, though Mrs Wix assures her it is branded so 'by the Bible' (Chapter XXVI). For when she had looked down from the inn-balcony on the café below, where 'the music of a man and a woman who, from beyond the precinct, sent up the strum of a guitar and the drawl of a song about "amour"', Maisie knew, the narrator adds impishly, 'what "amour" meant too, and wondered if Mrs. Wix did'. Maisie's French is advanced enough for her to be regarding this point as more than a matter of vocabulary. She is questioning the Puritanical view of sex. But she is not rushing to the other extreme. As Stuart Hutchinson pointedly asks, 'Who knows what Maisie means by her offer to meet Sir Clause at the "gold Virgin"?'[114] Is she implying romantic love or virginal protection from the consequences of his roving eye? A more plausible interpretation is that she is thinking of patience, of probation while waiting for affection to ripen into love, like the situation, presented without disapproval, in James's first novel, *Watch and Ward*. Maisie's expectations are not the real point, however (how could she be certain of any?). The crux is her insistence on Sir Claude's giving up his present mistress, Mrs Beale, whom Maisie does not trust. She is not so enamoured of an open relationship as to be willing to contemplate sharing with her. In the event, Sir Claude quite fails to come up to Maisie's mark on this issue, so the venture on to unchartered seas remains only a girlish might-have-been.

James handles actual sexual relationships in *What Maisie Knew* highly intelligently and sensitively, admitting both the power and drollery of sexual passion, while keeping firmly in view the pervasive need for decent concern for others, even

when choice has to be exclusive. Indeed it is this lesson, learned
by hard but never bitter experience, that the resilient Maisie
would wish to teach her parents. Taking a tolerant, but
discriminating line, she suggests that it may be possible to align
self-interest with benevolence, but it is all to little avail. The
earlier part of the novel is a wonderful exposure of human
egotism and casualness as they are temporarily confused by
futile impulses of natural feeling and guilt. The child acts as the
ideal register of the adults' moral weakness, being at once the
victim and the beneficiary in so far as she shuns bad examples.
Having the advantage of comparison, as she is shunted (in a
travesty of the Persephone myth) in half-yearly moves from one
unstable home to the other, Maisie is able to reach conclusions
beyond her years, though James carefully indicates her
limitations.

The English scenes in *What Maisie Knew* range from the
grotesque to the pathetic, as Maisie has to endure the sometimes
rough and sometimes soft treatment meted out to her by
her estranged parents and their various associates. The
characterisation has a special pointedness, appropriate to a
child's imaginative view of adults and amounting sometimes to
a Dickensian weirdness, especially in the case of the American
'Countess', 'a clever frizzled poodle in a frill or a dreadful
human monkey in a spangled petticoat' (Chapter XIX), who
gives her a handful of sovereigns. With regard to Maisie's
parents, the vivid physical imagery acts as an unforgettable
correlative for their irresponsibility towards her; for example,
'the wilderness of trinkets' on her mother's breast, where she
feels she has been suddenly thrust 'with a smash of glass'
(Chapter XV), or her father's 'shining fangs' amid 'the fragrance
of his cherished beard' (Chapter XVIII). There is not a
comparable Dickensian grip on the dialogue, where a character
as robust as Mrs Wix can lapse into the Jamesian abstract,
like 'What I want to speak of is what you'll *get* – don't you
see? – from such an opportunity to take hold' (Chapter XII).
But the alternation of impulse and calculation in all these
characters is firmly conveyed throughout. Such a sustained
presentation of inconsistency is bound to make for comedy, of
course, and, though the damage that could be done to Maisie is
frightening and serious, James's emphasis on Maisie's resilience
gives the novel buoyancy. Conceived as a child of native

intelligence, Maisie is shown as exercising courage and restraint. Without prejudice, vindictiveness or bitterness, she learns not to let her yearnings for a stable background, proper education and affectionate treatment show through. Fear of abandonment and cruelty occasionally dominates her feelings, but with the help of Sir Claude and Mrs Wix she develops to the point where she can judge the whole set with tolerance and realism.

Much of the wit of *What Maisie Knew* derives from the fact that neither of her rival governesses, the ostensibly charming Miss Overmore (later Mrs Beale) and the ugly Mrs Wix, is up to the task of bringing on so gifted a child. Mrs Wix, though she provides much-valued security, that 'tucked-in and kissed-for-good-night feeling' which the true mother had failed to deliver, has painfully 'little on facts' to impart to her pupil, even if her endless narratives enhance the girl's imaginative life (Chapter IV). Indeed, the very application of the term 'pupil' to Maisie is ironically sad, as are references to 'the interrupted students' (Chapter XI) and so on. Miss Overmore actually does more harm than good, or would do, if it were possible. Too intent on pursuing Maisie's father to do her duty in the schoolroom, she makes do with arch comments, which rebuke the girl's natural curiosity. For example, when Maisie asks if Sir Claude might become her tutor, so as to make his living with her mother right, 'as right as your being my governess makes it for you to be with papa', Miss Overmore, embracing her 'ingenious friend', is moved to protest:

> 'Of course not, he's ignorant and bad.'
> 'Bad – ?' Maisie echoed with wonder.
> Her companion gave a queer little laugh at her tone. 'He's ever so much younger – ' But that was all.
> 'Younger than you?'
> Miss Overmore laughed again; it was the first time Maisie had seen her approach so nearly to a giggle. 'Younger than – no matter whom. I don't know anything about him and don't want to', she rather inconsequently added. 'He's not my sort, and I'm sure, my own darling, he's not yours.' (Chapter VI)

The lady protests too much, we may say, and will soon be pursuing Sir Claude in lieu of her scheme of work. James catches excellently the hesitations with which Maisie's elders (but definitely not betters) convey to her intimations of their immorality, giving her more to go on than they intend. She uses words like 'live with' and 'lover' in a way which strikes them as guileful, when it is only mimetic and exploratory. Maisie's sense of fairness leads her to make false parallels, exposing the hypocrisy of the adults, until she doubts their reliability. Still wishing them different, she suffers from visions of their eventual misery in the heartless world they have joined. The anomalies which arise from her disproportionate sensitivity are both poignant and amusing.

What Maisie Knew is one of James's profoundest works, psychologically and morally, and can bear many rereadings. The scene in which Maisie's father, while apparently proposing to take her with him to America, is angling to have his second wife take complete responsibility for his daughter, is one of several finely balanced episodes. Maisie actually pities him for his embarrassment over his residual paternal feelings, yet so directed is her innocence 'towards diplomacy' that she is torn between 'alternatives of agreeing with him about her wanting to get rid of him and displeasing him by pretending to stick to him' (Chapter XIX). Even more vertiginous is her dilemma over her mother, whom she wants to help to be respected and loved, but who rejects her reminders and suggestions with appalling insults: 'You're a dreadful dismal deplorable little thing' (Chapter XXI). Even in her bafflement, Maisie retains her unruffled quality. James manages the free indirect style particularly well with Maisie, preserving her freshness and excitement without patronising her. Maisie's power of recovery is never lost sight of. Peter Coveney argues that this novel's morality is 'that of a human consciousness enriched by "innocent" acceptance of the squalid, developing an awareness of love and respect through their very absence and negation'.[115] Certainly Maisie comes to know love (she loves Sir Claude, almost from the first, as does Mrs Wix), but her discrimination is not just the wresting of a positive from a negative. James, through Maisie, makes it clear that, although sexual irregularity and trading with sex are often associated with coarse egotism, they are not to be identified with it. The power and use of sex have to be accepted as part of human relations. They are not necessarily 'squalid'. A 'moral sense' which deals in simple intuitions of moral beauty and squalor, such as Mrs Wix claims to have and blames Maisie for lacking, is inadequate to the more delicate exercise of conscience by which Maisie, with some faltering, lives. Maisie's suppressed tears at Boulogne station when she dares to think of going off alone with Sir Claude, tears which rise again in the hotel salon, have nothing to do with a 'moral sense', but with 'something still deeper' within her. Sir Claude calls it 'life . . . the most beautiful thing I've ever met – it's exquisite, it's sacred' (Chapter XXXI). It is that same feeling of hope, which can sting like conscience but is also tentative. It involves sacrifice, care, friendship, difficult choices, tolerance (but not impossible demands or indulgence) and openness to a changing future. Maisie thus emerges at the end of *What Maisie Knew* accepting what she knows, and still with a great deal to give.

James, having used the governess-figure in one way, as a source of information and as a protective, if limited, confidante, next used it in quite another way, to tell a ghost-story. In 'The Turn of the Screw' (*Collier's Weekly*, January–April 1898) the governess is the central consciousness, but in the autobiographical, confessional mode; the children here are innocent only in appearance, and the outcome turns not on what they become, but on what becomes of them. Orphaned, left by a rather indifferent guardian-uncle in the care of servants in his country-house at Bly, little Miles and Flora have been taken into the confidence of the former governess, Miss Jessel, and her lover, the guardian's former personal servant, Peter Quint, who subsequently both die and then continue to influence the children in evil ways. The governess-narrator encounters Miss Jessel and Quint in the form of particularly obnoxious ghosts. James is not concerned in 'The Turn of the Screw' with reality, except incidentally. It is clearly a fantasy-story. Since the governess's story both contains what could not have happened and proof that it did, it can logically be read in two contradictory ways, either as the genuine record of psychic experiences which the governess insists it is or as a deceptive, self-deceived invention. Since both interpretations are possible at once, there is little point in struggling to give one priority over the other. If the story were any more or any less credible it would lose its horrific fascination.

James deliberately established ambiguity in 'The Turn of the Screw' by means of the prologue, in which he feeds us through the narrator's friend, Douglas, information both on the governess's reliability and on her unreliability. She was inexperienced during her time at Bly, nervous, and intent on putting aside a sexual feeling for her employer, but she was a perfectly sane, trustworthy women after she had come through that time. Such intriguing ambivalence is atmospherically right for story-telling by the Christmas fireside. The prologue also sets the tale firmly in the early Victorian period, when fictional ghosts were in vogue. It introduces it as a contribution to a literary contest, of the tall-story order. Who can produce the grimmest horror-story 'on Christmas Eve in an old house'? The first use of the title is in connection with this competitive production. If in one such tale (the first of the three) the effect of a ghost appearing to a child rather than to an adult 'gives the effect another turn of the screw', what would be the effect of its appearing to two children, or indeed of two ghosts appearing to them? Douglas offers the company the governess's tale for crowning horror (it takes the prize, he means); 'For good uncanny ugliness and horror and pain ... It's beyond everything. Nothing at all that I know touches it' (prologue). The pressure applied by 'The Turn of the Screw' to listeners and readers comes, then, not from evidence of a real cruelty to children, like the harshness meted out in *What Maisie Knew*, but from frightening hints of a generalised, supernatural evil, into which the children have already been initiated. At the same time we are reassured that the governess had her first impression of that horror without losing her character.

The second use of the title in 'The Turn of the Screw' makes the point that, to preserve her integrity in repulsing the evil spirits, the governess had to employ her goodness as a means to an end. In order to maintain her equilibrium she blinded herself to the fact that the ghosts were 'revolting, against nature', and treated her ordeal as needing 'only another turn of the screw of ordinary human virtue' for the purpose of keeping up a 'fair front' (xxii). The governess is responsible for her own terminology, of course, Douglas presumably having borrowed from her account the phrase used in the title. Both uses of the title concentrate on strain, tension, weight, and assume a willingness to be involved with the horror. In one sense the governess's tale is her own character-reference, for she has to explain that what kept her in the presence of the ghosts was her proper desire to rescue the children from their influence.

James is at pains to remind us that the twenty-four chapters of the tale are a fictitious *written* account of the events at Bly. We are supposed to be given 'an exact transcript' of the governess's manuscript, written 'in old faded ink and in the most beautiful hand', the beauty of the hand finding an equivalent in the 'fine clearness' of Douglas's voice as he read the manuscript aloud. The narrative is full of self-conscious literary effects, beginning with the surprises which the governess received at Bly, making her 'think the proprietor still more of a gentleman' (i) than she had conceived on being appointed in Harley Street. As the plot thickens, the text makes apologetic references to itself: 'In going on with the record of what was hideous at Bly I not only challenge the most liberal faith – for which I little care; but (and this is another matter) I renew what I myself suffered' (ix). The pain and difficulty of writing the account come through intensely, doubling the unpleasant feeling: 'How can I retrace to-day the strange steps of my obsession?' (xiii). The answer to this question lies in the area of literary technique. The governess as writer is a reconstructor using her imagination: 'I again push my dreadful way through it to the end' (ix). She is not writing purely for herself (there is nothing to exorcise), but to impress others, as she had informed Mrs Grose, her housekeeper-friend who hardly knew what to believe. She has certainly read Ann Radcliffe's *The Mysteries of Udolpho* (1794) and probably *Jane Eyre* (1847), which contains the secret of 'an unmentionable relative kept in unsuspected confinement' (iv), which she evokes as analogies for her situation. There are also echoes of *Hamlet* – Quint's ghost, on the battlements of the tower, 'even as he turned away still markedly fixed me' (iii).[116] The governess's use of literary associations rather than pieces of evidence for psychical research does not mean that she is writing fiction, but it means that she gives the emotive priority over the descriptive. She evokes a great tradition of horror-writing to ensure gravity and the maximum conviction.

James himself discussed the reliability of the governess as a narrator several times.[117] He began, evidently, with the idea of the depraved and haunted children and then hit on the governess as an authoritative observer. The governess, while fully expressing her feelings at the time, keeps a clear record of the anomalies and obscurities which she observes at Bly, but, adds James, she does not necessarily give a clear explanation of them. Critics have inevitably wanted to fill this gap, perhaps the most ingenious explanation being that of C. Knight Aldrich, who maintains that Mrs Grose is the children's true mother and that she plots to drive the governess mad.[118] But the very idea of solving an enigma is foreign to the tone of 'The Turn of the Screw'. The peripheral mysteries, such as the cause of Miles's expulsion from school (probably trying verbal obscenities on boys whom he liked) or of Miss Jessel's death (possibly childbirth) give little trouble. The governess's delicacy could not stand very much explicitness in these matters. To take them too seriously is to miss the point of her own immense seriousness. Her main task as a character was to stimulate, not curiosity, but terror.

Whether James succeeded with her as a conveyor of terror depends largely on the language she uses. James's aim was clear enough: 'ah, the exposure indeed, the helpless plasticity of childhood that isn't dear or sacred to *some*body! That *was* my little tragedy.'[119] Fear for vulnerable children is as basic a human emotion as there is, and James boldly gives his narrator extremes of moral notation. Keeping in view the inexperience of 'a fluttered anxious girl out of a Hampshire vicarage' (prologue), who had had only a 'small smothered life' (iii), he has her admitting to herself a tendency to be prepared for romance and melodrama. She makes the contrast between the narrow, whimsical, gossipy world of her home village and the weird grandeur of Bly: 'I had the view of a castle of romance inhabited by a rosy sprite . . . Wasn't it just a story book over which I had fallen a-doze and a-dream?' (i). The whole bias of her style, based on eccentricity and reading, is towards exaggeration and polarisation. In this respect, 'The Turn of the Screw' is far from being an exercise in subtlety, but rather is a show of heightened colouring and strong reactions. The governess, while remembering to check herself, enthuses and condemns vehemently in the simplest of terms. The children, at first admired by her for their cherubic serenity, in which there was 'something divine' (iii), become later blacker than black. A 'premature cunning' appears in Flora's eyes, and Miles now must have been 'a fiend at school' (viii). Had 'the imagination of all evil' been opened up to him and had it flowered into an act? (xviii). But the governess's chief talent for lurid phraseology appears in her account of the apparitions, fed by Mrs Grosse's disapprobation of their terrestrial counterparts' behaviour, Quint's 'secret disorders, vices' (vi) and Miss Jessel's infamous liaison with him. The latter appears to the governess as her 'vile predecessor', to be addressed as 'You terrible miserable woman!' (xv) and characterised as a 'pale and ravenous demon . . . that wasn't in all the long reach of her desire an inch of her evil that fell short' (xx). Quint in his final manifestation, when Miles dies of shock, is purely Satanic, 'the hideous author of our woe' (xxiv). James exploits the Christian terminology appropriate to one from the governess's background for sensational, not theological, ends. As he recognises in the Preface to the New York edition volume, 'Peter Quint and Miss Jessel are not "ghosts" at all, as we now know the ghost, but goblins, elves, imps, demons as loosely constructed as those of the old trials for witchcraft.' He exploits demonological vocabulary to convey a general 'sense of the depths of the sinister' without giving examples of 'the imputed vice, the cited act'.[120] The reader is expected to supply these specifics privately.

Undoubtedly the reader of 'The Turn of the Screw' feels uneasy, with so much being vague and inexplicable, but there is another cause of bewilderment beyond the incidents and psychology, which is stylistic. The governess often slips into a sophisticated elusiveness which is disconcertingly remote from her moral bluntness. From this point of view there may be a third ghost in the story, that of Henry James himself, a ghost-writer directing the 'beautiful hand'. Ostensibly a historical novel of the 'It is sixty years hence' sort, the tale, having evoked its own historic atmosphere, slips erratically in and out of it. Thus the governess, who is capable of quaint things like 'an actor . . . never – no, never! – a gentleman' (v), can become elsewhere very difficult to follow, and when she perceives Flora's expression of detachment in 'a great childish light that seemed to offer it as a mere result of the affection she had conceived for my person' (ii). The accumulation of such unspoken thoughts, 'secret scenes', 'prodigious palpable hushes', 'I can call them nothing else – the strange dizzy lift or swim (I try for terms!) into a stillness, a pause of all life, that had nothing to do with the more or less noise we at the moment might be engaged in making' (xiii), certainly makes for tension, but it adds an unreal stylistic gloss to the period piece. Such disorientating shifts evoke the present in the past and reinforce the eeriness. The way in which the late Jamesian style haunts 'The Turn of the Screw' suggests its potential for dominating his last works. So pervasive a presence is the Jamesian style becoming that his central figures, from now on, have got to be thoroughly modern consciousnesses, intelligent, linguistically effusive, curiously observant. The style, while not limiting the characterisation, begins to influence the technique.

6

James the Modern Novelist – 'The Beast in the Jungle', *The Golden Bowl*

Henry James's early twentieth-century achievement, containing three great long novels and several masterpieces of shorter fiction, constitutes a challenge to all readers of literature. The paucity of incident and the narrowness of social range put some people off late James, and his imperfections of manner, amounting at times to preciosity, can be wearying during the long build-ups to the point. But for many devotees of the Novel, the late works are *the* ultimate reward, intriguingly revisitable, sure to yield pleasure and satisfaction in increasing amounts the more often they are read. No one need be surprised that Barbara Pym, for instance, when she was asked what book she would take to read on a desert island, chose *The Golden Bowl*.[121]

What makes these later novels of Henry James so notable is their almost unprecedented intensity of concentration on personal relations. As the main characters approach and negotiate major crises in these relations, the analysis of individual experiences reaches new heights of subtlety, and the prose flourishes with fine imagery, resonant allusion and precisely chosen vocabulary. The reader is continually aware of the artistic care which has gone into the selection of scenes for highlighting, the choice of characters for prominence at various stages, the control of information to be released and retained, and the pin-pointing of moments of entry, departure and reentry for the respective fictional consciousnesses. All this manipulation is James's, but James says hardly a word himself. James uses narration very much as a film-director uses the camera, or cameras; indeed, it is hard not to believe that James's experience of early cinematography influenced his technique in this regard. It is tempting to apply filmic terms like cutting, zooming and panning to his visual world. The telephone, too, may have influenced his dialogue, where interlocutors speak across a space of enigmaticalness, sometimes self-absorbed and expressionless, at other times confident of interpretation to the point of telepathy. Whatever the impact of modern technology on James, it is certainly not in the direction of crudity or popularity. His plots are predominantly intellectual; they are principally about the nature of truth, a truth that works both ways. The stories concern the discovery of truth about oneself and other people, sometimes good news, more often bad, the long process of awakening from deception, concealment and wishful thinking.

James was definitely modern in feeling the need to present the uncertainty of life and the modesty of the patterns which individuals can impose upon it. He had little hope of a markedly more orderly, just or rational future, based on science, politics or social theory. On the other hand, he did not hold that the violence, treachery and subversion which caught the headlines in his day and were to lead to the First World War were the ultimate significance of life or presaged some inevitable rebirth. James is a long way from cosmic despair and messianic utopianism. His principal characters totally lack facile assertiveness, but are shy, self-doubting types, the amiable Strether, the mortally ill Milly, the unsuspecting Maggie Verver. Such people are too intelligent for messages, creeds and nostrums. They are not too intellectual, however, to dismiss traditional morality; they worry when they cannot apply it to the situations which they face. They have some success, mixed though the results may be, in applying morality pragmatically. In their ongoing experience they balance principles against changing needs, relying on conscience as a check or as a warning that there is no further way forward down one particular path. Life is difficult in late James; his characters often cannot see the wood for the trees. They live, characteristically, away from home, attempting to find happiness, as Auden says, 'in another kind of wood',[122] ignoring memory or doubting its relevance. In the unfinished *The Sense of the Past* (1917), James suggests that to step back into the past is to hazard one's grip on the present life. His characters' consciousnesses dwell vividly in the present. James does not study families or households over the generations, concluding with young emancipated types confronted by a changed futurity. Too nervous for epic pretentions, he denies the reader the consolation of fictitious continuity in time and locality. Instead, James picks out the crowded months of life, the crises in the individual's awareness, the acceptance of compromise, loss, failure, departure, separation, uncertainty of outcome. The economy of subject combined with the elaboration of implication gives James's later works the quality of expanded short stories,[123] as indeed many of them actually are. If the artistry may seem too much for their content, it is not that the material is spun out beyond what its interest can bear, but that there is a certain contradictory interplay between James's own delight in shaping, patterning, dovetailing and symbolic paralleling on the one hand and his deep insight into the elusiveness and dense immediacy of life on the other. The unobtrusive skill of the author is all the more striking for the mercurial quality of the subject. The element of art looms large in James's later works, then, though not at the expense of 'felt life'.[124] The art is James's way of responding to life, partly assertive and brave, partly concise and restrained, and so contributes to our *sense* of life. In this connection, Virginia Woolf was right, surely, to accuse E. M. Forster of unfairness to Henry James in assuming an opposition between art and life in fiction; what, she asks,

> is this 'Life' that keeps on cropping up so mysteriously and so complacently in books about fiction? Why is it absent in a pattern and present in a tea party? Why, if we get a keen and genuine pleasure from the pattern in the Golden Bowl, is it less valuable than the emotion which Trollope gives us when he describes a lady drinking tea in a parsonage? Surely the definition of life is too arbitrary, and requires to be expanded.[125]

Life in the sense of liveliness, the proliferation of minor incidents and conversations, the to-ing and fro-ing of people in their walks of life, the amassing of contingent detail, what is called the slice of life, is, paradoxically, too narrow for James. The superficial sweep of ordinary realism is not expansive enough for him as a subject. Though James can display comic verve and dramatic tension, as in the Pocock chapters (XX–XXVII) of *The Ambassadors* (1903), the main development in that novel is in the life of the mind, the inner experience and changing attitudes of Strether. In *The Wings of the Dove* (1902) the effects which Milly Theale's enforced flight from life and protective extension of her wings of love and wealth have on the consciousness of Kate and Densher are the subject. The complication of changing personal relationships seen from different angles is the life which James succeeds in representing.

We are not given the impression that the pattern in a James novel is a 'cut-out' one, according to which characters keep on being the same, a formula for the novel's falling dead, according to D. H. Lawrence.[126] James is too aware of movements and shifts in his situations for that. For Lawrence, nevertheless, the ultimate test of a novel was its capacity to honour 'true and vivid relationships', of which the great one, for humanity, is 'the relation between man and woman', which will, he says, 'change forever, and will forever be the new central clue to human life'.[127] At this level, James, the eternal bachelor, might be thought to fail, perhaps through lack of intuitive audacity, perhaps because of distrust of generalisations. His lovers love either too late, or too clandestinely, or too possessively or too one-sidedly for James ever to honour love in the full Lawrentian sense. James does bring us to the brink of that, however, in *The Golden Bowl* especially, and he does a lot towards it by implication.

Probably the best explanation of James's unique gift as a novelist comes in L. C. Knights's essay, 'Henry James and the Trapped Spectator', in which James is said to release a 'sense of life' from a 'sense of suffocation' by means of 'operative irony': James's observers see the brutal truth of life too clearly for us to be able to say they evade it. Those sensitive, isolated individuals, aware of the general predicament of what Knights calls 'modern dishumanisation', nevertheless project a 'possible other case', by the extension of their observing intelligences, even though they themselves tend to be withdrawn from life.[128] The other case implied is often a what-might-have-been or what-could-be, even what-will-be. By relying on imaginative central figures, James stimulates imaginative responses in his readers. It says much for his penetration and his linguistic versatility that

James can project so much of positive value and interest from texts whose apparent drift is negative.

This ironic method is especially successful in 'The Beast in the Jungle' (*The Better Sort*, 1903), a story of fear, inhibition and desolation, which is nonetheless so finely balanced, controlled and expressed as to produce an almost exorcising effect. It deals with an unpromising character called John Marcher, a civil servant in his thirties, who keeps a low social profile, maintaining a theory of his 'being lost in the crowd' (i). He knows he has good but 'rather colourless' manners and wears 'the social simper' painted on a mask (ii). Marcher's problem is that a long while back he suffered a conversion to a kind of Hardyesque pessimism with a sharp personal application. He foresaw for himself 'a prodigious and terrible thing' happening that would 'perhaps overwhelm' him, 'possibly destroying all further consciousness, possibly annihilating me', or else altering everything for him (i). This prospect might well seem no more than the inevitable extinction which awaits all conscious beings, and Marcher admits that it is and will be natural, and not 'necessarily violent'. Nevertheless it makes him feel a haunted man, not only marked by fate, but different from others. James never suggests that Marcher is wrong in the general sense, only in his obsessive dramatisation of the blow to come. He invests it with some peculiar unknown awfulness, associating it with images of horror such as 'The Beast in the Jungle' and with a vague enigmaticalness, referring, for example, to 'dreadful unnameable things' (iv). Always waiting for the revelation of the form it will take, he is unable to concentrate on anything else. Ironically, though, since he is aware of the imbalance with which he pursues this preoccupation, Marcher is constantly on his guard against egotism, which he interprets as spreading his gloom to others. In particular, he is unwilling to contemplate marriage, since it would unsettle a woman to share his condition. That would be making claims.

Although in one sense the single-mindedness of Marcher in 'The Beast in the Jungle' is pointless, he is not presented by James as an eccentric. Outwardly reserved, he cultivates an extremely heightened form of the 'furnace-fear' of 'sure extinction' which rages in the speaker in Philip Larkin's 'Aubade', but without any similar appeal to common experience. Marcher broods without lucidity, remaining entirely passive 'in the hands of one's law' (ii). This subjection to a Victorian determinism turned morbid occurs in a post-Victorian social atmosphere compounded of philosophical indifference and material acquisitiveness. Marcher is acutely aware of the predatory nature of his fellow-guests at Weatherend, who eye the antiques with canine excitement, while preserving a tolerant, relaxed front: 'in such a life as they all appeared to be leading for the moment one could but take things as they came' (i). Marcher's sense of isolation is infuriating,[129] but it does not leave him unscrupulous, nor closed to unexpected developments. He is willing, guardedly, to renew his acquaintances with May Bartram, to whom, ten years previously, in Naples, he had divulged his secret apprehension.

The tale, highly original and entirely plausible, is the story of this relationship: May's devotion to Marcher and understanding of him until her death from what may be leukaemia and his simultaneous failure to understand until it is too late and to realise what he has missed by not giving her the love she deserved – all is filtered through Marcher's point of view. Marcher's failure to do May justice is kept constantly before us. His initial refusal to love keeps him blind to her need even while he is showing her every consideration: she is simply the right confidante for him, because of her 'consent not to regard him as the funniest of the funny' (ii). Year after year they discuss 'the topic' in her drawing-room, and he satisfies himself that she is not compromised by their habitual friendship, reflecting that her alliance with him is helpful as to his public image; 'to pass for a man like another' (iii). Marcher's unimaginative primness would be comic were it not so desolating.

An event which might well seem a blow from a savage universe then befalls not Marcher, but May, a cruel terminal illness, leaving Marcher alone to face the assault of remorse. Sadly, when the first signs of her debility manifest themselves, Marcher's main worry is only that May may die without ever having discovered the nature of the disaster by which *he* is doomed to be overwhelmed. But actually she has already guessed it. Then he is concerned lest 'the beast in the jungle' should prove to be no more than his having to witness the painful demise of his friend. With supreme insensitivity he betrays to May his alarm that he may in this way have been 'sold' or disappointed, a result entailing a 'drop of dignity' (iii):

he had wanted something more dramatic. However, Marcher's sense of his approaching loss is not so obtuse that it cannot be used by James to convey the effects of May's illness very movingly, without sentimentality or horror:

> He had gone in late to see her, but evening had not settled, and she was presented to him in that long, fresh light of waning April days which affects us often with a sadness sharper than the greyest hours of autumn. The week had been warm, the spring was supposed to have begun early, and May Bartram sat, for the first time in the year, without a fire, a fact that, to Marcher's sense, gave the scene of which she formed part a smooth and ultimate look, an air of knowing, in its immaculate order and its cold, meaningless cheer, that it would never see a fire again. Her own aspect – he could scarce have said why – intensified this note. Almost as white as wax, with the marks and signs in her face as numerous and as fine as if they had been etched by a needle, with soft white draperies relieved by a faded green scarf, the delicate tone of which had been consecrated by the years, she was the picture of a serene, exquisite, but impenetrable sphinx, whose head, or indeed all whose person, might have been powdered with silver. (iv)

The imagery of this passage, descriptive as well as figurative, fixes at once both May's grim plight and Marcher's blind vulnerability. He is still so driven by concern for his own enigma that he can compare May to something half-human. Apt though it is in several ways, the simile is wrong. He is only just beginning to recognise her indispensability to him. After her death Marcher recognises his own self-absorption and failure to respond to her love as something that 'profaned' the air (vi). There is perfect clarity at the end, when Marcher admits, possibly too harshly, that he had never thought of May 'but in the chill of his egotism and the light of her use' (vi). This bitter self-accusation does constitute the beast, which is exorcised in its ultimate assault when it is recognised as Marcher's own inner negativity. The theme of 'The Beast in the Jungle' anticipates that of William Golding's *Lord of the Flies* (1954).

The Golden Bowl (New York, 1904; London, 1905) is equally original, but denser than anything which even James had

written before. It stretches to forty-two chapters, which
characteristically can contain as few as five huge paragraphs of
psychological analysis. In order to expand the treatment of
mental life with such detailed notation (it can evoke comparison
with Proust and Joyce), James concentrates attention on four
characters. *The Golden Bowl* is basically about one marriage,
that of Maggie Verver to Prince Amerigo, and one affair, that
of Charlotte Stant, Maggie's friend, with the same Prince. The
complication, the marriage of Charlotte to Maggie's millionaire
father, Adam Verver, is treated mainly externally. A third
couple, the Assinghams, contribute much of the dialogue in the
form of a choric commentary on the others, with some
interference in the action also. The adjustments in these
relationships provide the material for virtually all the thought
and talk in the novel.

The golden bowl which gives the novel its title lacks some of
the mystique of other literary symbols, such as the rainbow and
the lighthouse. It has a double function, to suggest the inwardly
flawed but outwardly perfect relations of the principal quartet
and to serve as a recognition-device in the plot, whereby
Maggie discovers that Charlotte was intimate with Amerigo
before his marriage and, therefore, married her father with the
possibility of carrying on the liaison in mind. If both these uses
of the *objet d'art* seem a little mechanical, *The Golden Bowl* can
stand it; James develops the situation with low-key gradualism
and a discreet assumption of normalcy. There is rather more
plot to *The Golden Bowl* than one might expect, and at that level
it works well enough. But it is not the plot or the fate of the
bowl that provides the excitement.

Nor do the thematic patterns matter all that much in *The
Golden Bowl*. The usual theme of American innocence and
European experience undergoes a change when Maggie Verver
begins to acquire the wisdom of the serpent. The Italian
character, Amerigo, is a genuine study in aristocratic attitudes
in a somewhat *deraciné* type, whose reactions become increasingly
obscure. Charlotte, though born in Florence, is of American
origin, combining the conventional attributes of a beautiful
adventuress with a sacrificial reticence associated with New
World values. Fanny Assingham is another American type
abroad, the Society confidante, but I think one loses sight of
her nationality. The Ververs must seem recognisably American

in many respects, as James keeps suggesting. They exhibit 'the extraordinary American good faith' (Chapter I), which so amazes the Prince. Both seem easily deceived, yet are determinedly acquisitive. Mild and bland in manner, virtuously neat and smooth, yet quaint and modest, father and daughter achieve an amiability which falls short of charm. With the advantage of prodigious wealth, the Ververs exercise a steady power with a kind of slow cleverness, not doubting its ultimate irresistibility. Maggie, in particular, is one of James's most positive characters, turning the tables on her opponent with an ambiguous mixture of righteousness, pity and cruelty; 'the mixture of motive persists', as Sallie Sears expressively put it, 'though tempered always by Maggie's sense that she is primarily moved by moral considerations (however she may define them at a given time), and that she is not to blame if certain fringe benefits accrue to her in the process: such as having her husband helpless in a new alliance with her, such as the anguished humiliation and solitude of her enemy'.[130] Maggie's very concentration on success may seem typically American, as may other tendencies she shows with her father. There is their desire to surround themselves with beautiful collections to supply the aesthetic quality which they cannot themselves radiate. There is their moral conformism, which coincides with the promotion of their own interest, justifying their well-meaning arrangement of the concerns of other people. Also there is their conversational style of deceptively slow-witted analysis, which can issue in the most outrageous paradoxes. In these traits of the Ververs we may read a continuing Jamesian commentary on his fellow-countrymen. But the novel does not foreground such 'international' points, except fitfully.

The principal effects of *The Golden Bowl* are personal and intimate. The national and economic differences between Maggie and the Prince highlight but do not define the tension in their situation. It is not for nothing that James stages the action on the neutral ground of England – except for the scene where Charlotte accepts Adam, which is in Paris (Chapter XIII) – and never in Italy or in America. England provides a background of political power, opulent amenities, and social circulation which the Ververs can purchase as long-stay visitors, but it is not part of their lives. James, of course, contrasts the rich setting with the inner bewilderment and nervousness of the

characters. Their unhappiness is due, in the first place, to
Adam Verver's wealth and the Prince's need of it, but its core
lies inward, in wilfulness, audacity, fear. *The Golden Bowl* is
about ways of coming to terms with a situation which should
never have occurred. The eventual solution – separation – is as
painful as the strains which made it imperative.

How the situation arose is made adequately clear. The
Prince, amused by Fanny Assingham's matchmaking, agrees to
marry the Verver heiress, so that the 'rich peoples' could come
on to his side. Charlotte, not prepared to be left out, arrives
from America. Her opening gambit, 'You see you're not rid of
me. How is dear Maggie? (Chapter III) anticipates the whole
course of *The Golden Bowl*: Charlotte's inevitable presence and
Maggie's ambivalent state of mind. The Prince is well aware
that Charlotte's presence can have only one meaning, her
continuing love for him, or, as he puts it, 'the recurrent, the
predestined phenomenon, the thing always as certain as sunrise
or the coming round of Saints' days, the doing by the woman of
the thing that gave her away' (Chapter III). It is also
Charlotte's doom 'to arrange appearances', to which the Prince
contributes by not revealing to Maggie the nature of his
previous relationship with Charlotte (they 'had met constantly,
and not always publicly, all that winter', Chapter IV). This
failure in candour on the Prince's part is compounded by his
suggestion that Charlotte should marry 'some good, kind,
clever, rich American'. When Charlotte puts the point that she
could never love one, that there is no question of her adoring
one, the Prince replies, 'it's always a question of doing the best
for one's self one can – without injury to others' (Chapter III).
It is this apparently enlightened moral philosophy that the pair
try to apply without realising how easily injuries to others take
root and proliferate, unless scrupulously insured against in a
prudential way foreign to the Prince's Italian tradition and
emotionally resented by Charlotte. The concealment of the
relationship is already an injury to Maggie and the choice of
Adam for the 'good, kind, clever, rich American' a worse one,
especially since Maggie blindly encourages it. But Charlotte's
determination is fuelled by love, the only reciprocated passion
in the case, which vindicates it for her, and gives *The Golden
Bowl* its psychological balance. Love is the only one of
Charlotte's motives which is not mentioned in Fanny

Assingham's speculation with the Prince in Chapter II; Charlotte's wish to attend her old friend Maggie's wedding, her loneliness, her dislike of America, her lack of means, her impulsive generosity, all are considered, but not love. Yet love for the Prince (this time unreciprocated) also motivates Fanny herself: her sponsoring of the marriage with Maggie was her way of doing something for the Prince, at least financially. When Charlotte, then, enlists Fanny's aid in keeping quiet about the first of her outings with the Prince, she has the advantage: 'And you must help, dear . . . as you've helped, so beautifully, in such things before' (Chapter III). Fanny, in the first of many conversations on the situation with her more realistic husband, Colonel Bob Assingham, excuses herself by arguing that Maggie must never know evil, since she 'wasn't born to know evil'. Fanny even hopes that Charlotte will marry soon, to prove that she is cured, and will give Maggie support, by becoming 'an element of *positive* safety' (Chapter IV). But Bob Assingham is nearer the truth in backing Charlotte for knowing 'what she wants'. Charlotte is, in fact, to marry Adam Verver to get what she wants, freedom in her relationship with Prince Amerigo, to have something from him 'in all freedom', the only reason for which she would ever marry (Chapter VI). Fanny Assingham, as a party to the concealment, is drawn along by developments, wondering how to make the best of a bad job and not doing justice to the force of Charlotte's passion.

James's leisurely pace in *The Golden Bowl*, the very detail with which he approaches the characters' decisions and conversations, requires some time-gaps. The second part of the first half of the novel, narrated, surprisingly, from Adam Verver's point of view, deals with events two years after his daughter's marriage. It handles the continuing closeness between father and daughter, especially in their delight in the Principino, Maggie's baby son. Maggie, however, feels obscurely that there is a gap in her father's life, or perhaps should be, and Charlotte is induced to fill it. The coy manner in which Adam spells out to Charlotte the advantages and disadvantages of his offer, 'Of course I've worked it out – that's exactly what I *have* done' (Chapter XII), including Maggie's approval in his calculations, produces some of James's most uncomfortable comedy.

The third part, undoubtedly the most powerfully intense sequence in *The Golden Bowl*, brings the story a further two

years on, covering the full flourishing of Charlotte's affair with
the Prince, now her son-in-law by marriage. Although nothing
is explicitly admitted about the adultery, the meaning of their
affair is so overwhelmingly adulterous that both marriages seem
in retrospect to have been contrivances to facilitate it with the
comforts which the two could not themselves have afforded.
Maggie, accepting that Charlotte and her husband are more
suited to the social round than her father and herself, who so
love each other's company, extends an apparent 'understanding'
to their absence, as though, together, Charlotte and the Prince
can somehow 'represent' their respective spouses, even at a
country-house weekend party. It is a misunderstanding, not a
condonement, but under its protection Charlotte attains her
brief spell of happiness, and James rides high in presenting the
romance and audacity of it, as well as its droller aspects as a
very peculiar entanglement. Beginning the narration from
Charlotte's point of view and then modulating to that of the
Prince, James fills the episodes with corruscating social
descriptions, both lovers being conspicuous for their good looks,
high style and intelligent self-control. The opulent surroundings
are, at this point, enhanced, not undercut, by the feelings.
Charlotte's glimpse of the Prince at the Foreign Office reception
has this quality of transforming passion, when she has 'an
impression of all the place as higher and wider and more
appointed for great moments; with its dome of lustres lifted, its
ascents and descents more majestic, its marble tiers more
vividly overhung, its numerosity of royalties, foreign and
domestic, more unprecedented, its symbolism of "State"
hospitality both emphasised and refined'. For Charlotte, part of
the sweetness is her 'easy command, a high enjoyment, of her
crisis' (Chapter XIV). Crisis it is (in James every word counts),
but if Amerigo has his doubts, Charlotte supplies the 'highly
emphasized confidence' (Chapter XVII) and the courage.

It is not all brilliance in public, of course. When Charlotte
arrives at Portland Place, soaked, in a waterproof, 'invested
with the odd eloquence – the positive picturesqueness, yes,
given all the rest of the matter – of a dull dress and a black
Bowdlerised hat', her ironic indifference to her appearance has,
for the Prince, the effect of making the past meet the future,
'interlocking with it, before his watching eyes, as in a long
embrace of arms and lips' (Chapter XVII). James suggests the

sensual element in the relationship indirectly, and the permanence of the opportunity is questioned as it is affirmed. The lovers discuss the long day which Maggie and the child are spending with Adam Verver. The unnatural quality in the situation seems to taint those others rather than the lovers. Charlotte even suggests that had Adam been able to give her a child (he had not), it would only have brought him closer to Maggie; 'it would have taken more than ten children of mine, could I have had them – to keep our *sposi* apart' (Chapter XVIII). The lovers decide they must act in concert and trust each other, a vow sealed by a passionate kiss. But in this very commitment there is a hint of danger and magic, the 'tightened circle', the premonition of an 'abyss of divergence'. Excitement prevails; James had never used suspense so powerfully.

We wait, as Fanny Assingham's alarm grows while the visit of the lovers to Matcham and Gloucester is taking place. She is clearly wrong to insist, 'Nothing *has* happened. Nothing *is* happening.' Nevertheless she is right to note that Maggie is watching her father for the first sign that he has noticed anything untoward; 'Maggie's awake', Fanny observes (Chapter XXIV). It is a prelude to the second half of *The Golden Bowl*. James's long delay in introducing us to Maggie's point of view corresponds to her long sleep in the face of the double deceit playing around her. The plan now is for her to nullify the events which she has not noticed, to make Mrs Assingham's proposition that nothing has happened come true pragmatically. Charlotte's great love is to be frozen by silence and will-power.

The cooling of tone when we at last reach Maggie's view of the situation in Chapter XXV of *The Golden Bowl* is effected by the use of quaint imagery and exploratory syntax. After the ardent gestures of Charlotte and the sanguine gossip of Fanny Assingham, Maggie's 'inward voice' is chasteningly cautious, worried and dogged. The shift from the extravagant but straitened world of the lovers to the private, hesitant, infinitely penetrating and imaginative perceptions of the incongruously named Princess could hardly be more disconcerting. The sign of power, the conviction of rightness, emerges early in Maggie's assertion, the opposite of Fanny's, that 'Something *had* happened'; there had been a recent change in her life, but what? She was aware now of a concealed will at work in the situation, active irrespective of her own approval. Maggie's approach to the problem is compared, elaborately, with that of someone circulating in a garden round an 'outlandish pagoda', behind whose inscrutable surface a sound had now 'come back to her from within'. The exact bearing of this simile and others is hard to determine, except that they indicate a quality of detachment in Maggie which bodes ill for everyone else involved. She begins to study her husband experimentally by departing from her customary behaviour in 'small variations and mild manoeuvres' accompanied with 'an infinite sense of intention'. Not an entirely pleasant character, we feel, and the prose takes on a portentousness and a defining reticulation which is expressive of Maggie's alarmed seriousness and unwavering presence of mind. She forces the moves and does what she feels has to be done, the separation of the Prince from Charlotte, at an inevitable cost to her alliance with her father.

Maggie's plan is to confide her suspicions to Mrs Assingham and the Prince, but to say nothing to her father, thus leaving Charlotte in a torment of doubt. Sensing herself to have been managed up to this point, stifled 'in a bath of benevolence artfully prepared' (Chapter XXVI), she reciprocates. She proceeds 'with the application of her idea'; she translates 'her idea into action'; she proceeds 'consummately, for she felt it as consummate' (Chapter XXVII). Her strategy undermines the lovers' confidence; 'And that's how I make them do what I like!' (Chapter XXX). But it is an achievement close to despair, simply because Maggie now knows so much.

What makes the second part of *The Golden Bowl* so different from the first is the consideration that, whereas the passive characters then were unaware of the true significance of events, now Charlotte is bound to be alerted to her rival's manoeuvres. Maggie is thus conscious of Charlotte's suffering, whereas previously she had not been allowed to suffer herself, nor could she have suffered to the extent that Charlotte now does. Maggie has pity for the victim of her necessary unkindness; she feels for Charlotte in her invisible misery, which has to be borne behind a façade of social grace and wit. Maggie, when the Prince admits to her his long intimacy with Charlotte, realises that such love as theirs was inexorable (they 'had to' have their little hour together before her marriage and to deceive her subsequently, till she accidentally found out about it). But her own loyalty to her father is equally inexorable; she intends 'her care for his serenity, or at any rate for the firm outer shell of his dignity, all marvellous enamel', to be her 'paramount law' (Chapter XXXIV). The imagery suggests a hard, chilling, as well as an admirable quality, shared by father and daughter. It underlines that Maggie has to go to work without the quickness of a returned passion, but quite deliberately: she seems to see her husband 'hear her say even while her sounded words were other' that 'there may still be something in it for you – if you're capable of working with me to get that out'. There is little that is edifying here: the advantage is continued financial affluence and his wife's devotion, and the price is love, his refusal of Charlotte's. The Prince pays the price, is struck by Maggie's depth and persistence, but is slow to supply her with her want. Maggie's effort is primarily an exercise in damage-limitation and viability.

To bring off her *coup*, Maggie now has to practise duplicity on a grand scale, like a young actress, 'suddenly promoted to leading lady and expected to appear in every act of the five'. The Prince plays his part too, letting Charlotte alone, though she cannot let him alone. Maggie calls that 'an affair with which I've practically nothing to do', but her speculation on Charlotte's bruised feelings proves difficult to quell. She thinks of Charlotte as 'this unmistakeably mystified personage', her baffled consciousness bruising itself in a cage, 'the home of eternal unrest', from which she makes a 'grim attempt' at contact. 'The cage was the deluded condition, and Maggie, as having known delusion – rather! – understood the nature of cages' (Chapter XXXV). James's ironic pressure reaches the reader in increasing surges, as Maggie's campaign unfolds, for it is a fair comment on her feeling 'something like compassion' for Charlotte that Maggie knows of delusion in retrospect, whereas Charlotte's current misery is not so much delusion as the disappointment of overriding love. While only Maggie's point of view is registered, Charlotte's can also be assumed, and objectivity is maintained.

The conflict between these two American women in *The Golden Bowl* gives rise to some amazing scenes, notably the one after the bridge-party at Fawns, the Ververs' English country-house. Maggie has decided that she cannot merely rest there in outrage at having found 'evil seated, all at its ease, where she had only dreamed of good', but must act positively.[131] She who, in Fanny Assingham's view, had been born not to know evil is now the disillusioned idealist. But she has no intention of slackening the pressure on the others, of giving them up, that is, of letting them be. When Charlotte, joining her on the terrace, asks her if she is mistaken in thinking that there has been a change in Maggie's manner towards her, Maggie both lies and tells the truth simultaneously: Charlotte is mistaken in thinking Maggie has a grievance against her; 'You must take it from me that I've never at any moment fancied I could suffer by you' (Chapter XXXVI), and Charlotte responds by making her kiss her on it! Charlotte's cover is her imputation of jealousy to Maggie over her father, but Maggie, giving nothing away, has the upper hand, and plays it by using perfect ambiguity.

Charlotte's defeat comes when Adam agrees to remove himself and her to the hideous American City beyond the Mississippi, where his art-treasures are to be a benefaction to the municipality. Maggie, now secure, watches Charlotte's demeanour towards the collection of Fawns as a sign of what she will be doomed to do all her days over there. Charlotte marched the guests around, 'sparing them nothing, as if she counted, each day, on a harvest of half-crowns'. Maggie, however, can resist the temptation of vindictive satisfaction. Charlotte's high voice, praising *vieux Saxe* pieces as inestimable in value, strikes her 'like the shriek of a soul in pain' and actually makes her cry; the strange wail, 'Charlotte's high coerced quaver before the cabinets', repeats its inevitable echo (Chapter XXXVIII). The image of Charlotte as museum-guide carries poignant conviction. There may be worse fates, but would they make any difference? The ironic economy of James's narrative technique is just right here, for without the starch of Maggie's moral simplicity in the foreground Charlotte's plight would be a bit limp.

As it is, Charlotte carries off her departure dramatically, claiming to be surmounting the difficulty caused by Maggie's closeness to her father, 'since it's always with you that I've had to see him'. Open hostility is only just averted; Charlotte 'opened her sunshade with a click; she twirled it on her shoulder in her pride. " 'Ask' you? Do I need? How I see", she broke out, "that you've worked against me!"' whereupon Maggie ironically admits, 'What does it matter – if I've failed?' (Chapter XXXIX). Maggie has not overtly failed, since she needed to separate the lovers, but she has failed to avert loss, it is true. She is sensitive enough to be able to translate Charlotte's protest into its actual unspoken content:

> You don't know what it is to have been loved and broken with. You haven't been broken with, because in *your* relation what can there have been, worth speaking of, to break? Ours was everything a relation could be, filled to the brim with the wine of consciousness. (Chapter XL)

The romantic tone of this imputed speech marks Maggie's own longing rather than Charlotte's appraisal, which is not without prudence. The Prince may be right in pointing out that Charlotte will 'make her life' in American City with Adam, though his other reflection, 'Everything's terrible, *cara* – in the heart of man' (Chapter XLI), suggests that the nature of that life of Charlotte's remains unthinkable. Nothing is more impressive in James than the way his novels stop, making speculation as to the sequel somehow illicit. While bringing Maggie and the Prince together at the end of *The Golden Bowl*, James is careful not to make definitive statements about what has been achieved or where we go from here. The Prince does not accept that he sees what Maggie sees, ' "See?" I see nothing but *you*' (Chapter XLII), to which Maggie responds by feeling 'pity and dread' of his eyes and burying her own eyes 'in his breast'. As Ruth B. Yeazell argues, 'what we really witness here is less a closed fiction than a character struggling to will such a fiction'.[132] The omens are inscrutable. The flaws in the situation go back very deeply, and yet survival is possible in a fragmented state, as with the golden bowl itself.

The Golden Bowl is a remarkable case of the long exposition of a narrow subject, the private relations of a handful of characters almost royally detached from the rest of humanity. Even within these confines, James treads gingerly, so that in the second half, Maggie's half, the nature of the others' reactions, especially Adam's,[133] remains partly in doubt. Yet what it lacks in breadth, it makes up for in depth, stylistic fascination and, the Jamesian hallmark, ambiguity. After this *tour de force*, James looked to more familiar themes in his subsequent fiction, notably the *Doppelgänger* theme of 'The Jolly Corner' (*English Review*, December 1908) and the theme of friendship in retirement in

'The Bench of Desolation' (*Putnam's Magazine*, October–
December 1909 and January 1910), both curiously worked
stories. His final and unfinished novel, *The Ivory Tower* (1917),
promised a broad attack on the American rich and their
adherents in their extravagant Newport phase with a large cast,
including quaint and robust types. But this work, which would
have needed careful handling,[134] was abandoned at the outbreak
of the First World War, perhaps because James lacked the
compositional energy and power of selection to bring it off.

7
Henry James's Critical Fortunes

James's reputation held up fairly well in the years immediately following his death in 1916. With the Anglo-American-French-Italian alliance at its peak, James's presence as a friend of all four national cultures was still felt. James the 'character' was vividly remembered; anecdotes, tributes and biographical sketches predominated over critical assessments at this stage. Percy Lubbock's two-volume selection of the letters (1920) concentrated for much of its bulk on the period when James had ceased to publish novels. Mrs Humphry Ward in her reminiscences of James in *A Writer's Recollections* (1918) highlighted his interest in her own novels and said of his work that 'all through, the dominating fact is that it is "Henry James" speaking'.[135] James's personality was still a living force, evidently. The memorial numbers of *The Egoist* (No. 5, January 1918) and *The Little Review* (Vol. V, August, 1918), however, provided a first platform for younger writers to air their critical views of James. Both Ezra Pound and T. S. Eliot praised him in terms which went beyond respect for a distinguished predecessor. Eliot pronounced James 'the most intelligent man of his generation'. He insisted that, despite the successful realism of many of the characters, James's focus was not on character, plot or ideas, but the 'focus is a situation, a relation, an atmosphere',[136] a formulation which may have discouraged attempts to clarify James's subtlety and elusiveness, but which certainly drew attention to his originality. Pound's remarks were more downright, conveying a clear sense of James's moral grip. Pound designated James as 'the hater of tyranny', the opponent of 'all the sordid petty personal crushing oppression, . . . the impinging of one personality on another: all of them in highest degree damn'd, loathsome and detestable'. But Pound's special enthusiasm was for James's international quality; he wished justice to be done to James's 'striving in every way to bring in America on the side of civilization', for James's art was 'a struggle for communication', which is 'a recognition of differences, of the right of differences to exist, of interest in finding things different'.[137] Pound's view of James as an intellectual liberal, concerned with central humane issues and dedicated to enhancing understanding between peoples, has a wartime ring to it, but reverberates even today as honest and necessary.

Few writers are invulnerable to negative judgments once their deaths have passed out of the news some way. Critical fashion in the 1920s was unfavourable to most pre-war work, including James. James's concentration on fine points of conduct among the comfortably-off seemed complacent to those whose memories of mass wartime horror and deprivation were indelible. Masters of violence and crime like Dostoevski and Conrad looked to them more prescient than James. The sparer prose of post-war American writers like Gertrude Stein and Hemingway made James's expressiveness appear an excess. The move to a more explicit presentation of sexuality in fiction, associated especially with D. H. Lawrence, left James looking unnecessarily discreet. The frank bedroom scenes in *The Rainbow* (1915) seem an age away from the unnarrated encounter of Kate and Densher in *The Wings of the Dove* (1902), which in the 'prime afterglow' can be traced only atmospherically in the latter's Venetian lodgings (Book 9, Chapter I). Proust and Joyce also, while having something in common with James in their representation of the languid, idle consciousness playing over experience and memory, are too preoccupied with trivial detail, learned allusion and sexual grotesquerie to claim a continuity with the older writer, for whom redundancy was itself unclassical. The scene in Joyce's *Ulysses* (1922), in which Bloom contemplates his genitals in the bath, 'the dark tangled curls of his bush floating, floating hair of the stream around the limp father of thousands' ('The Lotus-Eaters'), has a jocularity and studiousness quite foreign to James. I think it is clear now that, for all their audacity and perseverence, the moderns of those days are outstripped by James in the power of both irony and economy. But then he seemed dated. The stream-of-consciousness method, in the van of literary taste in the 1920s, would have been too messy and wasteful for James, but felt radical and spontaneous in an age of experiment. James's analyses were thought too timid, his dialogue too strained, his descriptive prose too formal and sedate. All misjudgments, but outspokenness ruled. Doubts, voiced earlier,[138] renewed themselves: were the obscurity and ambiguity of so much of Henry James worth the effort?

In America Van Wyck Brooks added a nationalist note to the disapproval by arguing in *The Pilgrimage of Henry James* (1925), a work of unguarded sarcasm, that exile in Europe had so destroyed James's sense of objective reality that the last novels were no more than 'exhalations of intellectual vapour, those nebulae'.[139] Then E. M. Forster in *Aspects of the Novel* (1927) directed a broadside at James on the level of novel-theory, an area where he might have been supposed to be least vulnerable. James's disciple Percy Lubbock had erected James's point-of-view technique as the central tenet of his *Craft of Fiction* (1921), but Forster challenged this high estimate: he argued that James might have achieved artistic consistency, but only at the expense of life, for the artistic path pursued by James was a narrow one, requiring the sacrifice of the number and variety of his characters. His people were, believed Forster, 'incapable of fun, of rapid motion, of carnality, and of nine-tenths of heroism. . . . Maimed creatures can alone breathe in Henry James's pages – maimed yet specialized'.[140] Images of war are getting between Forster and James here, but the attack, bluff and unfair as it was, swept the field clear of James-supporters for a time. Edwin Muir, following in Forster's wake in *The Structure of the Novel* (1928), went so far as to dismiss the Jamesian novel as a 'minor offshoot' of the tradition of fiction, a tradition which, incidentally, also had no room for George Eliot and Conrad.[141] The low point is reached with Orlo Williams, who reported in 1928 that nobody read James any more owing to changes of attitudes induced by the war in the previous decade.[142] The explanation of this disregard was, according to Williams, that James had sacrificed the direct treatment of the passions to the cause of aesthetic form. A Jamesian obsession with aesthetic unity is now being adduced as an artificial restriction, excluding from his novels not only types of people, incident and experience but also deep feeling. If both ideas and emotions are absent from

James, we may wonder what is left. Some kind of attenuated personal relations? Even that residue is denied him by V. Louis Parrington, who in *The Beginnings of Critical Realism in America* (1930) maintains that James's cosmopolitanism left him flavourless and aloof from homely realities:

> From the external world of action he withdrew to the inner world of questioning and probing; yet even in his subtle psychological enquiries he remained shut up within his own skull-pan. His characters are only projections of his own brooding fancy, externalisations of hypothetical subtleties.[143]

James, for Parrington, is a self-deceived romantic and a forerunner of expressionism. When James is regarded as a *total* subjectivist, criticism itself seems to have lost touch with objective reality. Perhaps the popularity of works like 'The Turn of the Screw' was turning to James's disadvantage; one can see the relevance of Parrington's strictures to, say, *The Sense of the Past*, but even here the tale itself criticises the notion of self-absorption. In connection with works replete with irony, like 'Daisy Miller' or *Washington Square*, where the author's stance is hard to discover, Parrington's accusation is impossible to sustain.

It was, in fact, with a revival of interest in such early works that the rehabilitation of James's writings began. American academic interest naturally centred on his native origins and affinities with other nineteenth-century novelists. Cornelia P. Kelley's *The Early Development of Henry James* (1930) was a pioneering work in this area, inaugurating the study of James as a reviewer and critic. Constance Rourke in her *American Humor* (1931) took up hints from Eliot, mentioning James's links with Hawthorne and Poe as well as the comparison with Mark Twain:[144] 'No American before him had made a full imaginative approach to living characters and the contemporary scene.' The importance of the early works was stressed by Stephen Spender for a further reason, their parallels with James's own later works, since both deal with Americans abroad and observe a social system in decay. At the same time Spender noted the English influence on James: *The Princess Casamassima* is praised as being in the tradition of Dickens and Thackeray.[145] Spender's essay, 'The School of Experience in the

Early Novels', was contributed to a special James number of *Hound and Horn* (edited by Lincoln Kerstein, April–June 1934), which included noteworthy articles by Marianne Moore (on James's Americanness), Edmund Wilson (on his ambiguity) and R. P. Blackmur (on his theory of the novel). In the editorial 'homage' to James, another contributor, Edna Kenton, whose essay of ten years earlier, 'Henry James and the Ruminant Reader' (*The Arts*, 6), influenced Wilson's idea of Jamesian ambiguity, is described as 'the first Jacobite of America',[146] a sure sign that the James cult is already underway.

The seriousness of the new commendation of James in the later 1930s is attested by the value placed on his treatment of evil. In a period when the menace of a fanaticism more ingenious and powerful than any known for centuries was impinging on everyone, James's status rose steadily. James's presentation of evil, whether in the form of sexual corruption, of manipulation of the weak by the strong or of smug, materialistic unscrupulousness, was now felt as the iron hand in the velvet glove. Hugh Walpole asserted in 1932 that by intellect and temperament James was 'an explorer, ceaselessly inquisitive, aware of all the darkest and most morbid corners of the human heart'.[147] Newton Arvin noted that James's vision was of a world morally as ugly 'as any in the English novel, up to that point',[148] and Graham Greene contended sternly not only that James was driven to write by 'a sense of evil religious in its intensity' but also that his characters, who form the immoral background to the 'period of haphazard violence'[149] which preceded the First World War, placed him beside Shakespeare in the unpitying analysis of corruption. War is now an aid, rather than a hindrance, to the understanding of James's themes. During the Second World War William Troy explained the fact of James's current appeal by the depth of the metaphysical panic and moral despair through which James had passed in order to assert a humanist sense of continuity with the dead: 'At a moment when loss of continuity is our gravest threat, when personality is everywhere at a discount, when all consequent values dissolve in the general terror, it is probably no great wonder that more and more people are turning to Henry James'.[150] Even in this neo-apocalyptic paean there is still an acknowledgement that James's greatest strengths are negative. Yvor Winters in 1937 argued that James's Puritan-

derived moral sense was too vulnerable to avoid being 'dissolved
in air' when brought up against European conventions.[151]
Edmund Wilson, however, had argued that James, in 'his shy,
circumlocutory way', was genuinely democratic, preserving in
his characters all that was 'human, magnanimous, reviving in
the new American spirit'; Wilson admitted, of course, that
James effected his contact with life, 'not at close quarters, but
through long, infinitely sensitive antennae'.[152] It was L. C.
Knights in his 'Henry James and the Trapped Spectator' who
advanced this discussion the furthest by demonstrating that
James's narrative technique was a form of deep irony. For
Knights, James's moral sense is both vital and satiric: he has a
full command of villainy, egoism, brutality and self-
righteousness, even though his observer-characters are detached
from the world which they see so clearly; the implication is
always hopeful and valid, not debilitated and disabled.[153]
Knights's exposition of the link between serious content and
subtle technique in James opened the way for many more
sophisticated analyses of the texts.

During the mid-century period James criticism was dominated
by F. R. Leavis, who characteristically trenchantly defended his
preferences among the novels. Leavis's views on James were
known to Knights before the publication of the 'Trapped
Spectator' essay from a review of Blackmur's *The Art of the Novel*
in *Scrutiny* (vol. 5; March 1937). Leavis was to incorporate this
review in his chapter on Henry James in *The Great Tradition*
(1948), where James is placed with Jane Austen, George Eliot
and Joseph Conrad as one of the 'great English novelists', to
whom D. H. Lawrence was to be added as a fifth. Leavis's
main point is that James's 'registration of sophisticated human
consciousness is one of the classical creative achievements',
producing 'an ideal civilized sensibility'.[154] He identifies as
James's best work in this kind *The Europeans, Washington Square,
The Portrait of a Lady, The Bostonians, The Awkward Age* and *What
Maisie Knew*, as well as several tales and certain strands in other
novels, like the Kate Croy parts of *The Wings of the Dove*. Leavis
insisted, however, that James had less grip on reality and
rendered it with less specificity than George Eliot at her best;
he saw *The Portrait of a Lady* as dependent on the Gwendolen
Harleth parts of *Daniel Deronda*, and as more evasively inexplicit
than that: 'The difference between James and George Eliot is

largely a matter of what he leaves out'. Returning to Yvor Winters' idea of James's moral sense as concerned with free choice, free from economic necessity, Leavis decides that James's work is comparatively limited in human interest and that the 'strenuously refined art' is a compensation in itself, a compensation, which only lasts until 'the hypertrophy of technique' sets in.[155] There is no admission that James's ironies may be strategic. Leavis believes that interest in James inevitably turns into interest in James's 'case', by which he means the decline into wordiness and preciosity; 'it seems to me obvious that the "case" becomes in some places boring to the point of unreadableness', and if others disagree Leavis suspects a 'tacit conspiracy'[156] to admire those works where 'something certainly did go wrong', a fault which he describes as an unsureness in the 'moral touch'. In the later James, Leavis may wish for more obvious moral discrimination. He sees no irony, for instance, in the presentation of the Ververs in *The Golden Bowl*; apparently James 'had no inkling' of any element of distaste in his readers for the Ververs' arrangement of the situation. But, one must object, surely the distaste is realised in Charlotte. Leavis does not fully appreciate the impersonality of the 'dramatic' method in later James. He complains that James 'did not live enough' and could not even at his best simply express 'rich and free first-hand living', rather a romantic objection. Though Leavis ends disarmingly by affirming that it is a mark of our sense of the greatness of James's genius 'that discussion should tend to stress mainly what he failed to do with it',[157] he really has exaggerated the gaps. Leavis engages acutely and candidly with James, especially on points of style, but it is difficult not to conclude that his strictures are too severe. But every point Leavis makes needs to be answered. His successful effort to get the earlier and shorter James works which he preferred accepted, against the odds, as current classics did indeed do much more for James than the blander recommendations of contemporary critics, such as F. O. Matthiessen in *Henry James: The Major Phase* (1944). The sharpness of Leavis's arguments brought James into the centre of critical debate, so that more patient evaluations of James's objectivity and subtlety in the devalued works inevitably emerged in the long run.

The securing of James's position as a major author in English and American literature some thirty years after his death has led to a proliferation of scholarly and expository activity. Most of his writings are currently in print in cheap and increasingly reliable editions. There is no complete edition of the novels, but James's tales, plays, letters, essays and reviews have all been edited with varying degrees of fullness. Biographical studies include Leon Edel's admirably readable five-volume *Life* (1953–70). James's stories are frequently adapted to the stage, cinema and television. No single critical trend has predominated during the last four decades, but in the sketch of recent academic work on James which follows, I group some of the outstanding books according to such patterns as seem discernible.

The post-war era began auspiciously for James studies with F. W. Dupee's collection of secondary material, *The Question of Henry James* (1945), in the introduction to which James was praised for having a classical conception of the imagination as the 'organiser and intensifier of life', to which he appropriated 'those features of empiricism which stress the importance of concrete experience and the value of method'.[158] Dupee's *Henry James* (1951) in the American Men of Letters series set the tone for the James criticism of the 1950s by drawing attention to James's background. Marius Bewley in *The Complex Fate* (1952) placed James in an American literary tradition including Cooper, Melville and Hawthorne which already stressed the interconnection of American and English cultures. Quentin Anderson's *The American Henry James* (1957) put the emphasis on Henry James's father's influence and argued for the existence of Swedenborgian symbolism in the later works. Christof Wegelin, however, kept Europe to the fore in his *The Image of Europe in Henry James* (1958), for without his European experience, he argues, James would not have come to terms with the American character.

The 1960s saw an ever-widening amount of new criticism on James, often over a hundred articles and a dozen dissertations a year. The decade began with complementary studies on James's liberating sense of comedy (R. Poirier, *The Comic Sense of Henry James*, 1960) and on James's idea of evil as restricting and static (J. A. Ward, *The Imagination of Disaster*, 1961). Outstanding among the critical achievements of this period is Oscar Cargill's *The Novels of Henry James* (1961), a systematic synthesis and review of all scholarly comment so far made on James's novels.

It was joined in 1966 by S. Gorley Putt's *A Reader's Guide to Henry James*, which covers the short stories as well. Studies which select a handful of texts for elucidation of James's moral and aesthetic preoccupations and narrative techniques included Dorothea Krook's *The Ordeal of Consciousness in Henry James* (1962), Sister M. C. Sharp's *The "Confidante" in Henry James* (1963), L. B. Holland's *The Expense of Vision* (1964) and Ora Segal's *The Lucid Reflector* (1969). Almost alone at that time, Maxwell Geismar maintained the hostile note common in the 1920s; his *Henry James and his Cult* (1964) accused academic critics of overpraising James and argued that James's method worked against possibilities of freedom in the novel as a form. Walter Isle, however, maintained in *Experiments in Form* (1968) that, at least in the period 1896–1901, James's developing fictional techniques moved in the direction of typical twentieth-century experiments. Studies of a more specialist nature at that time included Robert L. Gale's *The Caught Image* (1964), on the density of the imagery, Naomi Lebowitz's *The Imagination of Loving* (1965), on personal relations, Sallie Sears's *The Negative Imagination* (1968), on the tension between events and their doubtful significance, and Peter Buitenhuis's *The Grasping Imagination* (1970), which linked the novels to James's non-fiction writing on America.

A reemergence of the British critical interest in James became clear in 1972 with John Goode's *The Air of Reality*, nine essays by various writers on James's mimetic power, discussing his representation of such items as social deference, money, girls' training and the theatre. Money is also the subject of D. L. Mull's *Henry James's 'Sublime Economy'* (1973). Kenneth Graham's *Henry James: The Drama of Fulfilment* (1976) is a lively appreciation of presentational skill in James, dwelling on his flair for scenes and climaxes, and Brian Lee's *The Novels of Henry James* (1979) explores the influence of cultural change on the characters' minds. Alwyn Berland, in *Culture and Conflict in the Novels of Henry James* (1981), establishes James's intellectual debt to the Victorian sages, whereas W. R. Veeder, in *Henry James: The Lessons of the Master* (1975), has stressed the links with Victorian popular fiction. S. Donadio, in *Nietzsche, Henry James, and the Artistic Will* (1978) links James's pursuit of a transforming and redeeming art back to the Transcendentalists. A number of recent critics concentrate on another side of James's efforts, his

affinities with the Modernists; among them are S. B. Purdy
(*The Hole in the Fabric*, 1977), S. Perosa (*Henry James and the
Experimental Novel*, 1978), and S. Hutchinson (*Henry James: An
American as Modernist*, 1982). Studies which apply modern
linguistic-critical ideas of 'reading' to James include N.
Bradbury's *Henry James: The Later Novels* (1979) and S.
Kappeler's *Writing and Reading in Henry James* (1980). New post-
structuralist, Marxist and Historicist critical essays on James
are collected in Ian F. A. Bell's *Henry James: Fiction as History*
(1984), a feminist perspective is provided by Virginia C. Fowler's
Henry James's American Girl (1984), and the politics of the novel
forms the subject of Mark Seltzer's *Henry James and the Art of
Power* (1984). The diversification of these discussions can be
expected in work still in progress and in articles in numerous
current journals, most notably in *The Henry James Review* (1979 –
continuing). Critical absorption in James shows no sign of
becoming outmoded, though the terms of discourse have
inevitably altered. James's position at the parting of two
centuries and the confluence of two literatures, English and
American, no doubt ensures his attractiveness to contemporary
critics of a wide variety of persuasions. His own critical
awareness and contribution to novel-theory also guarantee his
prominence. The sense in which a James novel requires the
reader's special cooperation is another commendation in today's
climate.

Of direct influence from James on later novelists it is more
difficult to speak. James's world did not immediately die with
him. Apart from members of his own circle like Edith Wharton,
any sensitive novelist who handles the international theme or
shows a child's view of a sophisticated group or dwells on a
character's subjective view, like Elizabeth Bowen, L. P. Hartley
or Henry Green, may be said to follow in his steps. James's
preoccupation with form looks forward to Virginia Woolf, with
dialogue to I. Compton-Burnett, with narrational stance and
selection of incident to Conrad and Graham Greene. Other
traditions have more bearing on each of these novelists than
James's, however. They are post-Jamesian authors, rather than
Jamesian, except here and there. Inasmuch as after him all
novelists have probably consciously decided whether they are
using point-of-view technique or not and if they are going to

leave some facts ambiguous or not, James's example is pervasive. But diffused too; the novel has fissured into so many fragments since James's day that there is no one practising today who could seriously be called a disciple.

Still, a similar statement could have been made about Shakespeare a hundred years after *his* prime. James's greatness is not quite of that order, but it looms larger with distance in time. The density and precision of his prose, the duration of his career and volume of his productions, the clarity of his characters, the mixture of tragic and comic intuitions in his plots, the humanity, wit and independence of his attitudes, together all these features lift him above even his most distinguished contemporaries and compatriots. He sets standards in irony, judgment, restraint and subtlety, especially in the denotation of people's thoughts. He who can, for instance, convey Kate Croy's view of her father with this awesome vividness and flexible rhythmic and stylistic control has a mastery of wit and grimness which it is hard to match:

> No relation with him could be so short or so superficial as not to be somehow to your hurt; and this, in the strangest way in the world, not because he desired it to be – feeling often, as he surely must, the profit for him of its not being – but because there was never a mistake for you that he could leave unmade, nor a conviction of his impossibility in you that he could approach you without strengthening. He might have awaited her on the sofa in his sitting-room, or might have stayed in bed and received her in that situation. She was glad to be spared the sight of such penetralia, but it would have reminded her a little less that there was no truth in him. This was the weariness of every fresh meeting; he dealt out lies as he might the cards from the greasy old pack for the game of diplomacy to which you were to sit down with him. The inconvenience – as always happens in such cases – was not that you minded what was false, but that you missed what was true. He might be ill and it might suit you to know it, but no contact with him, for this, could ever be straight enough. Just so he even might die, but Kate fairly wondered on what evidence of his own she would some day have to believe it. (*The Wings of the Dove*, Book 1, Chapter I)

It is the kind of passage every reader wants to analyse, revisit, discuss, make much of, recommend.

In American literature, then, James is the first; he may be outpointed in single works or parts of works by other Americans, but there is no one there to approach him in quantity of excellent work. In English literature he ranks below our very greatest writers: he is not as versatile as Shakespeare, not as poised as Jane Austen, not as funny as Dickens, nor as candid as D. H. Lawrence, but I would put him above all the rest, including the poets, the Irish and the moderns – the exception is George Eliot, whose sense of community he certainly lacked, though he is, for all that, just ahead of her in intelligence; I cannot easily separate those two. In world literature Henry James must count for more than any ancient or neoclassical writer; he is more varied than Cervantes, more interesting than Stendhal, Flaubert and Proust, more balanced than Dostoevski and more brilliant than Fontane and Mann. Certainly he must yield place to Dante, Goethe and Tolstoy, but after them and the English authors I have named he comes, in my view, next.

Notes

1. James's first American heroine, Lizzie Crowe in 'The Story of the Year' (*Atlantic Monthly*, vol. XV, March 1865), practises Beethoven and Chopin piano pieces and reads Goethe's *Faust* in German. James's first critical work, the review of Nassau Senior's *Essays on Fiction* (*North American Review*, vol. XCIX, October 1864), praises Scott in cryptically 'advanced' terms as a parrier of questions who is improvident of the future: Scott is the ideal chronicler who produces 'self-forgetful' fictions which undertake to prove 'nothing but facts', pp. 585–7.

2. L. Edel (ed.), *Henry James Letters*, vol. I (London: Macmillan, 1974), pp. 132–3; letter to Alice James, 31 August 1869.

3. *Ibid.*, vol. IV (Cambridge, Mass. and London: The Bellknap Press of Harvard University Press, 1984), p. 466; letter to William James, 17 October 1907.

4. L. Edel, *Henry James: The Untried Years, 1843–1870* (London: Rupert Hart-Davis, 1953), pp. 42 and 91.

5. L. Edel (ed.), *Henry James Letters*, vol. IV, p. 770; letter to H. G. Wells, 10 July 1915.

6. L. Edel, *Henry James: The Untried Years*, pp. 90–103.

7. Henry James, *A Small Boy and Others* (London: Macmillan, 1913), p. 227.

8. *Ibid.*, pp. 1–3.

9. F. O. Matthiessen, *The James Family* (New York: Knopf, 1947), pp. 321 and 339.

10. Mrs Humphry Ward, *A Writer's Recollections* (London: Collins, 1918), pp. 326–7.

11. L. Edel, *Henry James: The Conquest of London, 1870–1883* (London: Rupert Hart-Davis, 1962), p. 67. As late as 1897 after a visit to Old Place, Linfield, James found the whole thing 'far too Germanic, too Teutonic, a business to make a medium in which I could ever sink down in peace'. The elements of France and Italy were, to James, 'the real secret of Style'. MS letter to Lady G. Wolseley, 8 March 1897, Hove Central Library.

12. Henry James, *A Small Boy and Others*, p. 231.

13. Harvard MS letter of Henry James senior, quoted in Matthieson, *op. cit.*, p. 88.

14. Henry James, *Notes of a Son and Brother* (London: Macmillan, 1914), p. 4.

15. L. Edel (ed.), *Henry James Letters*, vol. I, p. 26; letter to T. S. Perry, 18 July 1860.

16. Henry James, *Notes of a Son and Brother*, p. 110.

17. See the record of a conversation which James had with his nephew, Henry James junior, in 1913, and a letter to T. S. Perry in which it is clear that James dropped two of the transatlantic crossings from his narrative in the autobiography, in L. Edel, *Henry James: The Untried Years*, pp. 140–2.

18. Harvard MS, quoted in L. Edel, *Henry James: The Untried Years*, p. 203.

19. L. Edel (ed.), *Henry James Letters*, vol. I, p. 77; letter to T. S. Perry, 20 September 1867.

20. *Ibid.*, vol. III (London: Macmillan, 1980), p. 17; letter to Elizabeth Boott, 11 December 1883, and vol. II (London: Macmillan, 1978), p. 314; letter to Grace Norton, 7 November 1880.

21. R. H. Super (ed.), *Philistinism in England and America* (*The Complete Prose Works of Matthew Arnold*, vol. X, Ann Arbor, Michigan: University of Michigan Press, 1974), p. 7.

22. See Roger Gard, *Henry James: The Critical Heritage* (London: Routledge and Kegan Paul, 1968), pp. 75–7 for the Hutton review (*The Spectator*, 5 July 1879, vol. LII, pp. 854–5) and pp. 4–9 and p. 548 for discussions of the reception of James's novels and their sales.

23. L. Edel (ed.), *Henry James Letters*, vol. II (London: Macmillan, 1978), pp. 274–5; letter to T. S. Perry, 22 February 1880.

24. L. Edel, *Henry James: The Conquest of London*, p. 327.

25. F. O. Mathiessen and K. B. Murdock (eds), *The Notebooks of Henry James* (New York: Oxford University Press, 1947), pp. 27–8; entry for 25 November 1881.

26. L. Edel (ed.), *Henry James Letters*, vol. III, p. 67; letter to Grace Norton, 24 January 1885.

27. *Ibid.*, p. 244; letter to William James, 19 October 1888.

28. L. Edel (ed.), *Guy Domville, Henry James* (London: Rupert Hart-Davis, 1961), pp. 212–13; from H. G. Wells's 'A Pretty Question' (*Pall Mall Gazette*, 7 January 1895, p. 3).

29. L. Edel (ed.), *Henry James Letters*, vol. IV, pp. 510–15; letters to G. B. Shaw, 20 and 23 January 1909.

30. *Ibid.*, p. 34; letter to E. Gosse, 28 August 1896.

31. Henry James, *The Ivory Tower* (London: Collins, 1917), p. 259.

32. R. P. Blackmur, *The Art of the Novel: Critical Prefaces, by Henry James* (New York: Scribner, 1934), p. 52.

33. See my *The Ambassadors*, Unwin Critical Library (London: Allen and Unwin, 1984), pp. 151–2.

34. L. Edel (ed.), *Henry James Letters*, vol. IV, p. 353; letter to E. Gosse, 16 February 1905.

35. See Stuart Culver, 'Representing the Author: Henry James, Intellectual Property and the Work of Writing', in *Henry James: Fiction as History*, ed. Ian F. A. Bell, Critical Studies Series (London, and Totowa, N.J.: Vision Press and Barnes and Noble, 1984 and 1985), pp. 114–36. Culver argues that James was increasingly 'concerned with how literature functioned in the general economy'; he takes issue with writers who have interpreted

James's mask of masterdom as a symbol of anti-commercial, aesthetic isolationism; *op. cit.*, p. 134, and notes 20 and 21, p. 136.

36. Ford Madox Ford, *Thus to Revisit: Some Reminiscences* (London: Chapman and Hall, 1921), pp. 118–19.

37. Ford Madox Ford, *Henry James: A Critical Study* (London: Secker, 1913), p. 9.

38. H. G. Wells, *Boon* (London: Fisher Unwin, 1915), p. 108.

39. L. Edel (ed.), *Henry James Letters*, vol. III, p. 36; letter to T. E. Child, 8 March 1884.

40. Review of Turgenev's *Frühlungsfluthen* and *Ein König Lear des Dorfes*, *North American Review*, vol. CXVIII (April, 1874), pp. 355–6.

41. L. Edel (ed.), *Henry James Letters*, vol. II, p. 339; letter to Mrs Henry James senior, 7 February 1881.

42. P. Lubbock (ed.), *The Letters of Henry James*, vol. II (London: Macmillan, 1920), p. 161; letter to T. B. Saunders, 17 January 1910.

43. L. Edel (ed.), *Henry James Letters*, vol. IV, p. 606; letter to T. S. Perry, 21 March 1912.

44. *Ibid.*, p. 642; letter to H. C. Andersen, 28 November 1912.

45. P. Lubbock (ed.), *The Letters of Henry James*, vol. II, p. 410; letter to William James junior, 31 August 1914.

46. See S. Nowell-Smith, *The Legend of the Master* (London: Constable, 1947), p. 166.

47. *The New York Times Magazine*, 21 March 1915, p. 4.

48. L. Edel, *Henry James: The Master, 1901–1916* (London: Rupert Hart-Davis, 1972), pp. 533–5.

49. From an anonymous review of *A Passionate Pilgrim, and other Tales* (1875), in *Atlantic Monthly*, vol. XXXV (1875), 490–5; reprinted in R. Gard, *Henry James: The Critical Heritage*, pp. 31–4; where the editor notes that it may be by W. D. Howells.

50. The sonnet, 'Written in Butler's Sermons', was first published in Arnold's *Poems* of 1849. The essay, 'Bishop Butler and the Zeit-Geist' is in R. H. Super's edition of *Essays Religious and Mixed* (The Complete Prose Works of Matthew Arnold, vol. VIII, Ann Arbor, Michigan: University of Michigan Press, 1972), pp. 11–62.

51. Henry James, *Partial Portraits* (London and New York: Macmillan, (1888), p. 7. The essay 'The Life of Emerson' first appeared in *Macmillan's Magazine*, vol. LVII (December 1887), pp. 86–98.

52. R. P. Blackmur, *The Art of the Novel: Critical Prefaces*, p. 35. James's later, somewhat guilty, view of the turning-point of *The American*'s plot as an experience 'uncontrolled by our general sense of "the way things happen"' (*op. cit.*, p. 34) may be influenced by Edith Wharton's disillusioned grasp of French aristocratic priorities, as displayed in her *Madame de Treymes* (1907), which he read before composing the Preface (1907) to the New York edition of *The American*.

53. This phrase is used by Arnold in 'Numbers' (*Nineteenth Century*, April 1884; in Super, *Philistinism in England and America, ed. cit.*, vol. X, 1974, p. 155), but already in *Literature and Dogma* (1873), Chapter XI, 4, Arnold had argued that the French respect for equality had as its weaker side a tactful making

the most of 'the average sensual man' and a promoting of the 'pleasurable life of Paris' (Super, *Dissent and Dogma, ed. cit.*, vol. VI, 1968, pp. 390–1).

54. F. R. Leavis, *The Great Tradition* (London: Chatto and Windus, 1948), p. 142. Leavis regards Newman as one of a line of symbolic American figures who lack the corruptions of European culture and represent for James 'energy, uncompromising moral vitality and straightforward will'. Much of the criticism voiced by Newman of French society is indeed valid.

55. In *The Middle Years* (London: Collins, 1917), p. 82, James describes how Lewes returned *The Europeans* to its lender with the unflattering words, 'Ah those books – take them away, please, away, away!'

56. James told Elizabeth Boott, possibly exaggerating, 'You are quite right to hate Gertrude, whom I also personally dislike!', L. Edel (ed.), *Henry James Letters*, vol. II, p. 190; letter to Elizabeth Boott, 30 October 1878.

57. That James wrote the scenes and dialogues in *The Europeans* from a standpoint influenced by Matthew Arnold is confirmed in the letter he wrote to his father on 25 March 1878 (*Henry James Letters*, vol. II, p. 162), praising Arnold's essay on 'Equality' in the *Fortnightly Review* (vol. XXIX) for that month as 'charming'. 'I cannot get over a feeling of pleasure that he writes just as he does; even his limitations have a practical excellence.' In 'Equality' Arnold draws attention to the disadvantages in America's having had 'social equality before there has been any such high standard of social life and manners formed' as there had been in France by the old nobility. On the other hand, this same aristocracy was now out of its element in estimating the power of current ideas and beauty: 'They may imagine themselves to be in pursuit of beauty; but how often, alas, does the pursuit come to little more than dabbling a little in what they are pleased to call art, and making a great deal of what they are pleased to call love!' (Super, *Essays Religious and Mixed, ed. cit.*, vol. VIII, 1972, pp. 288 and 301). Figures like Mr Wentworth and the Baroness Munster are complex, sympathetic fictional portraits, underpinned by general observations like Arnold's.

58. P. J. Eakin in *The New England Girl* (Athens, Georgia: University of Georgia Press, 1976) traces the embodiment of Puritan and Transcendentalist ideas in Mrs H. B. Stowe's and W. D. Howell's fictional characters as well as in Hawthorne's.

59. L. Edel (ed.), *Henry James Letters*, vol. II, p. 179; letter to William James, 23 July 1878.

60. W. D. Howells, *Heroines of Fiction* (New York: Harper, 1901), vol. II, p. 165.

61. L. Edel (ed.), *Henry James Letters*, vol. II, p. 166; letter to Henry James senior, 19 April 1878.

62. James may have known Julia Newbury from Chicago, described as 'sprightly, full of opinions, naive, talkative, and a real charmer', who died suddenly in 1876 at the age of twenty-two in Rome and was buried in the Protestant cemetery; see M. Aziz (ed.), *The Tales of Henry James*, vol. 3, 1875–1879 (Oxford: Clarendon Press, 1984), pp. 15–16.

63. R. P. Blackmur, *op. cit.*, p. 269.

64. *Ibid.*, pp. 187–8.

65. *Ibid.*, p. 269.

66. L. Edel (ed.), *Henry James Letters*, vol. II, p. 304; letter to Mrs Eliza Lynn Linton, August 1880.

67. E. Wagenknecht argues strongly that Daisy Miller is neither a rebel nor a martyr: see his *The Tales of Henry James* (New York: Ungar, 1984), p. 17.

68. 'Americans Abroad', *Nation*, vol. XXVII (3 October 1878), pp. 208–9.

69. R. P. Blackmur, *op. cit.*, pp. 207 and 198.

70. *Ibid.*, p. 193.,

71. S. G. Putt, *A Reader's Guide to Henry James* (London: Thames and Hudson, 1966), p. 123.

72. Review of *Washington Square*, in *The Spectator*, vol. LIV (5 February 1881), p. 186. 'There is no doubt that it is genius, and genius of the most marked order, genius for painting character, and genius for conceiving unalloyed dismalness of effect, without tragedy and without comedy.' See R. Gard, *op. cit.*, p. 90.

73. Notably by Graham Greene, who refers to 'the delicate, feline *Washington Square*' as 'perhaps the only novel in which a man has successfully invaded the feminine field and produced work comparable to Jane Austen's' ('Henry James: The Private Universe' in D. Verschoyle's *The English Novelists* (London: Chatto and Windus, 1936), p. 219). P. Buitenhuis, in *The Grasping Imagination: The American Writings of Henry James* (Toronto: University of Toronto Press, 1970), p. 108, argues that 'in this novel, if anywhere, if can be claimed that James was a kind of male Jane Austen'.

74. L. Edel (ed.), *Henry James Letters*, vol. II, p. 316; letter to William James, 27 November 1880. *Fouillé* means 'elaborately detailed, thoroughly probed'.

75. The theory of John Lucas, in his essay *'Washington Square'*, in *The Air of Reality: New Essays on Henry James*, ed. J. Goode (London: Methuen, 1972), pp. 44–5.

76. D. W. Jefferson, *Henry James and the Modern Reader* (Edinburgh and London: Oliver and Boyd, 1964), p. 107.

77. L. Edel (ed.), *Henry James Letters*, vol. II, p. 315; letter to Grace Norton, 7 November 1880.

78. Ezra Pound, 'A Shake Down', in *The Little Review*, vol. V, August 1918, No. 4, p. 13. 'Autochthonous' means 'indigenous', native to the place.

79. L. Edel, *Henry James: The Conquest of London, 1870–1883*, p. 387.

80. L. Edel (ed.), *Henry James Letters*, vol. II, p. 193; letter to William James, 14 November 1878.

81. R. B. Perry, *The Thought and Character of William James* (Boston: Little Brown, 1935), vol. I, p. 380; letter to William James, 16 December 1879.

82. L. Edel, *Henry James: The Conquest of London*, p. 404.

83. *Ibid.*, p. 373.

84. R. P. Blackmur, *op. cit.*, p. 48.

85. Graham Greene, Introduction to the World of Classics edition of *The Portrait of a Lady* (London: Oxford University Press, 1947), p. vi. O. Cargill, in *The Novels of Henry James* (New York: Macmillan, 1961), p. 91, adduces Edmond About's *Germaine* (1858) as the source for Madame Merle's exploitation of Isabel in order to provide for her illegitimate child.

86. Stuart Hutchinson, in *Henry James: An American as Modernist* (London and Totowa, N.J.: Vision, and Barnes and Noble, 1982 and 1983), argues

that James himself 'engages us *within* the experience of the book, but not alongside it' and that his 'irony must finally be very much the irony of identification' with Isabel, since James, like Isabel, is a modern American, 'exiled from traditional sureties, affronting uncertainty', pp. 26 and 38.

87. E. Wagenknecht, in *The Novels of Henry James* (New York: Ungar, 1983), rightly stresses Isabel's power to retaliate; 'it is quite clear that she is not a broken woman', p. 86.

88. L. Edel, Introduction to the Torchbook Edition of *The Tragic Muse* (New York: Harper, 1960), p. xii.

89. R. P. Blackmur, *op. cit.*, p. 223.

90. See R. Posnock, *Henry James and the Problem of Robert Browning* (Athens, Georgia: University of Georgia Press, 1985), pp. 83 and 209, n. 17. Posnock's discussion of the possibility that James was troubled by the ease with which Browning combined a married life with a successful poetic career, though it begs the question as to how successful James judges Browning's poetry to be, is particularly illuminating with regard to James's 'The Lesson of the Master' (*Universal Review*, July and August 1888) and 'The Private Life' (*Atlantic Monthly*, April 1892).

91. K. Graham, in *Henry James: the Drama of Fulfilment* (Oxford: Clarendon Press, 1975), p. 72. He affirms that a 'note of the bizarre and even of the playful is always compatible with the most serious activity of James's imagination', p. 58. He gives an impressively detailed account of the stylistic and narrative virtuosity of 'The Aspern Papers', though I do find his enthusiasm for the 'swelling hoard' of the papers themselves, that 'magic compendium and totem' (p. 65), exaggerated.

92. See Susanne Kappeler, *Writing and Reading in Henry James* (London: Macmillan, 1980), p. 55, for a discussion of the narrator's discourse as being 'under suspicion' on these matters, as in a court case.

93. See R. C. McLean, '"Poetic Justice" in James's "Aspern Papers"', in *Papers on Language and Literature*, vol. III (1967), pp. 260–6, p. 264, and E. Wagenknecht, *The Tales of Henry James* (New York: Ungar, 1984), pp. 224–5, notes 8 and 9, for details of this debate.

94. Wayne C. Booth, *The Rhetoric of Fiction* (Chicago: University of Chicago Press, 1961), pp. 341–64.

95. Ora Segal, *The Lucid Reflector: The Observer in Henry James's Fiction* (New Haven, Conn.: Yale University Press, 1969), p. 91.

96. R. P. Blackmur, *op. cit.*, p. 168.

97. *Ibid.*, p. 164.

98. J. I. M. Stewart, *Eight Modern Writers* (Oxford: Clarendon Press, 1963), p. 98.

99. R. P. Blackmur, *op. cit.*, p. 89. See my '*The Tragic Muse*: The Objective Centre', *Journal of American Studies*, vol. IV, pp. 73–89 (July 1970) for a discussion of James's presentation of Miriam Rooth.

100. Granville Hicks, in *The Great Tradition: An Interpretation of American Literature since the Civil War* (New York: Macmillan, 1933), p. 115, argues that Nick Dormer's political career never seems a real alternative to the artist's life 'for the reason that the political life of England is never presented to us as a comprehensible and important form of human activity'.

101. R. P. Blackmur, *op. cit.*, p. 219.

102. F. O. Matthiessen and K. B. Murdock (eds), *The Notebooks of Henry James*, pp. 148–9; entries for 3 and 9 February 1894.

103. R. P. Blackmur, *op. cit.*, p. 221.

104. S. Kappeler, *op. cit.*, pp. 83 and 85.

105. L. Edel (ed.), *Henry James Letters*, vol. III, pp. 507–8; letter to William James, 9 January 1895. See also L. Edel, *Henry James: The Treacherous Years, 1895–1900* (London: Rupert Hart-Davis, 1969), pp. 59–74.

106. F. O. Matthiessen and K. B. Murdock (eds), *op. cit.*, pp. 188 and 208; entries for 14 February and 11 August 1895.

107. *Ibid.*, pp. 263 and 254; entries for 21 December and 19 February 1896.

108. *Ibid.*, p. 136; entry for 24 December 1893.

109. R. P. Blackmur, *op. cit.*, pp. 300 and 129–32.

110. F. O. Matthiessen and K. B. Murdock (eds), *op. cit.*, p. 248; entry for 13 February 1896.

111. See especially P. F. Quinn, 'Morals and Motives in *The Spoils Of Poynton*, *Sewanee Review*, vol. LXII (1954), pp. 563–77; E. L. Volpe, 'The Spoils of Art', *Modern Language Notes*, vol. LXXIV (1959), pp. 601–8; R. C. McLean, 'The Subjective Adventure of Fleda Vetch', *American Literature*, vol. XXXVI (1964), pp. 12–30; and Sister M. C. Sharp, *The Confidante in Henry James* (Notre Dame, Ind.: Indiana University Press, 1963). Ch. 4. The last argues that it is 'Fleda's goodness of character that suffuses the picture with a pleasant glow', p. 109.

112. F. R. Leavis is right to note that, though *The Spoils of Poynton* contains 'much that is strikingly good', James 'has not been closely enough controlled by his scheme of essential significance' in it, but has over-developed 'partial interests'. See *The Great Tradition*, p. 141, n.

113. James W. Gargano, in '*What Maisie Knew*: the Evolution of a "Moral Sense"', in *Nineteenth-Century Fiction*, vol. XVI (1961), pp. 33–46, p. 34, points out that the very idea that Maisie was proposing to become Sir Claude's mistress was never suggested before 1956. See Harris W. Wilson, 'What did Maisie Know?', *College English*, vol. XVII (1956), pp. 279–81; her greatest asset . . . is her virginity, and that she is prepared to offer', p. 281.

114. Stuart Hutchinson, *Henry James: An American as Modernist*, p. 70.

115. Peter Coveney, *The Image of Childhood* (Hardmondsworth: Penguin, 1967), p. 200. This study, a revised edition of his *Poor Monkey* (London: Rockliff, 1957), has an introduction by F. R. Leavis, who disagrees with the author over the suggestion that *What Maisie Knew* 'skirts dangerously close to something akin to "obscenity"'. Leavis argues that the thrill is only for 'poor conventionally moral Mrs Wix', but not for the reader, because of the separation of Maisie from the adult world; pp. 25–6 and 205. The idea that Maisie's 'rather admiring way' of 'prying into the sexual lives of her very promiscuous elders' had 'something particularly obscene' in it came from Stephen Spender's 'The School of Experience in the Early Novels', in *Hound and Horn*, vol. VII (1934), pp. 417–33; p. 432.

116. *Cf. Hamlet* I, i ('Mark it, Horatio') and I, ii ('And fix'd his eyes upon you?' . . . 'Most constantly').

117. Recording the story (from a lady) related by the Archbishop of Canterbury, E. W. Benson, to James early in January 1895, James called it a 'ghost-story' in which wicked servants corrupt young children, die and then

return to haunt and try to get hold of them – 'The story to be told – tolerably obviously – by an outside spectator, observer'. *The Notebooks of Henry James*, pp. 178–9; entry for 12 January 1895. Having written 'The Turn of the Screw', he explained to several correspondents that the thing was a pot-boiler, intended to convey terror. For example, see L. Edel (ed.), *Henry James Letters*, vol. IV, p. 86: 'The grotesque business I had to make her picture and the childish psychology I had to make her trace and present, were, for me at least, a very difficult job, in which absolute lucidity and logic, a singleness of effect, were imperative. Therefore I had to rule out subjective complications of her own – play of tone etc.; and keep her impersonal save for the most obvious and indispensable little note of neatness, firmness and courage – without which she wouldn't have had her data', letter to H. G. Wells; 9 December 1898. In the Preface to the New York edition, however, James added that it had been a matter of 'our young woman's keeping crystalline her record of so many intense anomalies and obscurities – by which I don't of course mean her explanation of them, a different matter', R. P. Blackmur, *The Art of the Novel: Critical Prefaces by Henry James*, p. 173.

118. C. K. Aldrich, 'Another Twist to "The Turn of the Screw"', *Modern Fiction Studies*, vol. XIII (1967), pp. 167–78; pp. 175–6.

119. L. Edel (ed.), *Henry James Letters*, vol. IV, p. 84; letter to L. Waldstein, 21 October 1898.

120. R. P. Blackmur, *op. cit.*, p. 175.

121. Barbara Pym, *A Very Private Eye* (London: Macmillan, 1984), p. 318; letter to Philip Larkin, 27 July 1978.

122. W. H. Auden, 'In Memory of W. B. Yeats' (1940), l. 20.

123. F. R. Leavis felt that the explanation of the word-spinning in *The Ambassadors* was 'that it had been conceived as a short story', which James was 'so mistakenly led into fluffing out . . . to the bulk and pretensions of a major work'. 'Henry James and the Function of Criticism', *Scrutiny*, vol. 15 (Spring 1948), pp. 98–104; p. 100, reprinted in *The Common Pursuit* (London: Chatto and Windus, 1952), p. 225.

124. R. P. Blackmur, *op. cit.*, p. 45.

125. Virginia Woolf, 'Is Fiction an Art?', *New York Herald Tribune*, VII, 16 October 1927, p. 6.

126. D. H. Lawrence, 'Why the Novel Matters', in *Phoenix*, ed. E. D. McDonald (London: Heinemann, 1936), pp. 533–8; p. 537.

127. D. H. Lawrence, 'Morality and the Novel', *The Calendar of Modern Letters*, vol. II(December 1925), pp. 269–74; pp. 272–3.

128. L. C. Knights, 'Henry James and the Trapped Spectator', *The Southern Review*, vol. IV (Winter 1939), pp. 600–15; pp. 64–7. See also R. P. Blackmur, *op. cit.*, p. 222.

129. E. Wagenknecht in *The Tales of Henry James* (New York: Ungar, 1984), p. 148, sees Marcher as 'the empty man with whom literature since James's time has become so tiresomely preoccupied, the embodiment of what Hemingway called "Nada", the man "to whom nothing on earth was to have happened", and this he becomes through his inability to love'. His refraining from love is, however, well-motived and, later, sharply regretted.

130. S. Sears, *The Negative Imagination* (Ithaca, N.Y.: Cornell University Press, 1968), p. 215.

131. Jean Gooder tends to overstress Maggie's 'feverishly absorbed introspection' when she states, 'The problem is that with no check outside Maggie's meditations we cannot be sure whether she is divining or inventing'. There *is* a check in what the others say and in what we remember from the first half of the novel, and even in herself she tries to see both sides. See '*The Golden Bowl*: Ideas of Good and Evil', in *The Cambridge Quarterly*, vol. XV (1984), pp. 142–4.

132. R. B. Yeazell, *Language and Knowledge in the Late Novels of Henry James* (Chicago: Chicago University Press, 1976), p. 125.

133. V. C. Fowler's view that Adam's connoisseurship is so acquisitive as to be dehumanising in its effect upon others, so that Maggie's struggle for selfhood involves her inevitable rejection of him, is worth considering in this context. See V. C. Fowler, *Henry James's American Girl* (Madison, Wis.: University of Wisconsin Press, 1984), pp. 136–8.

134. See my '*The Ivory Tower*: The Cessation of Concern', *Journal of American Studies*, vol. X (August, 1976), pp. 241–55.

135. Mrs Humphry Ward, *A Writer's Recollections*, p. 336. She admires the *wealth* of James's work, 'the deep draughts from human life that it represents . . . and there is scarcely anything in human feeling, normal or strange, that he cannot describe or suggest'.

136. T. S. Eliot, 'In Memory', in *The Little Review*, vol. V (August 1918), No. 4, pp. 45–6.

137. Ezra Pound, 'Brief Note', in *The Little Review*, vol. V (August 1918), No. 4, pp. 7 and n., and 9.

138. Notably by W. C. Brownell, who doubted if to the majority of intelligent readers the difficulty of the later writing did not need 'an amount of effort disproportionate to the sense of assured reward', in 'Henry James', *Atlantic Monthly*, vol. XLV (April 1905), p. 518, and more amusingly by H.G. Wells in *Boon*, p. 108.

139. Van Wyck Brooks, *The Pilgrimage of Henry James* (New York: Dutton, 1925), p. 141.

140. E. M. Forster, *Aspects of the Novel* (London: Arnold, 1927), pp. 205–6.

141. Edwin Muir, *The Structure of the Novel* (London: Hogarth Press, 1928), p. 12.

142. Orlo Williams, '*The Ambassadors*', *Criterion*, vol. VIII (September 1928), p. 50.

143. V. L. Parrington, 'Henry James and the Nostalgia of Culture', in *Main Currents in American Thought*, vol. III, *The Beginnings of Critical Realism in America (1860–1920)* (New York: Harcourt Brace, 1930), pp. 239–41.

144. Constance Rourke, *American Humor: A Study of the National Character* (New York: Harcourt Brace, 1931), p. 262.

145. Stephen Spender, 'The School of Experience in the Early Novels', *Hound and Horn*, vol. VII (April–June 1934), p. 431.

146. Lincoln Kerstein, 'Homage to Henry James 1843–1916', *ibid.*, p. 362.

147. Hugh Walpole, *The Apple Trees: Four Reminiscences* (Waltham St. Lawrence: Golden Cockerel, 1932), p. 58.

148. Newton Arvin, 'Henry James and the Almightly Dollar', *Hound and Horn*, vol. VII, p. 437.

149. Graham Greene, 'Henry James', in D. Verschoyle (ed.), *The English Novelists* (London: Chatto and Windus, 1936), pp. 213–28; pp. 215–16.

150. William Troy, 'The Altar of Henry James', *The New Republic*, vol. CVIII (15 February 1943), pp. 228–30; p. 230.

151. Yvor Winters, 'Henry James and the Relation of Morals to Manners', *American Review*, vol. IX (October 1937), pp. 483 and 490.

152. Edmund Wilson, 'The Ambiguity of Henry James', *Hound and Horn*, vol. VII, pp. 405 and 398.

153. L. C. Knights, 'Henry James and the Trapped Spectator', *The Southern Review*, vol. IV (Winter 1939), pp. 600–15.

154. F. R. Leavis, *The Great Tradition*, pp. 1 and 16.

155. *Ibid.*, pp. 110 and 111.

156. *Ibid.*, p. 17.

157. *Ibid.*, pp. 127, 159, 160, 163 and 172.

158. F. W. Dupee (ed.), *The Question of Henry James: A Collection of Critical Essays* (London: Allen Wingate, 1947), p. viii.

Bibliography

JAMES'S PRINCIPAL WRITINGS

NOVELS

Watch and Ward (1871)
Roderick Hudson (1875)
The American (1876–7)
The Europeans (1878)
Confidence (1879–80)
Washington Square (1880)
The Portrait of a Lady (1880–1)
The Bostonians (1885–6)
The Princess Casamassima (1885–6)
The Reverberator (1888)
The Tragic Muse (1889–90)
The Other House (1896)
The Spoils of Poynton (1896) (first published as 'The Old Things')
What Maisie Knew (1897)
The Awkward Age (1898–9)
The Sacred Fount (1901)
The Wings of the Dove (1902)
The Ambassadors (1903)
The Golden Bowl (1904)
The Outcry (1911)
The Ivory Tower (1917)
The Sense of the Past (1917)

COLLECTIONS

(i) Prose Fiction

The New York Edition of the Novels and Tales of Henry James (New York: Scribner, 1907–9), 24 vols (2 more vols added in 1918).
The Novels and Stories of Henry James, ed. P. Lubbock (London: Macmillan, 1921–3), 35 vols.

The Complete Tales of Henry James, ed. L. Edel (London: Rupert Hart-Davis, 1962–4), 12 vols.
The Tales of Henry James, ed. M. Aziz (Oxford: Clarenden Press, 1974) 3 vols continuing.

(ii) Plays

The Complete Plays of Henry James, ed. L. Edel (Philadelphia and New York: Lippincott, 1949).

(iii) Essays

James, Henry, *Hawthorne* (London: Macmillan, 1879).
James, Henry, *Partial Portraits* (London and New York: Macmillan, 1888).
James, Henry, *Notes and Reviews* (Cambridge, Mass: Dunster House, 1921).
The Art of the Novel: Critical Prefaces, by Henry James, with an introduction by R. P. Blackmur (New York: Scribner, 1934).
James, Henry, *The Scenic Art*, ed. A. Wade (New Brunswick: Rutgers University Press, 1948).
James, Henry, *The American Essays*, ed. L. Edel (New York: Vintage, 1950).
The Painter's Eye: Notes and Essays on the Pictorial Arts by Henry James, ed. J. L. Sweeney (London: Rupert Hart-Davis, 1956).
James, Henry, *Parisian Sketches*, ed. L. Edel and I. D. Lind (New York: New York University Press, 1957).
The House of Fiction: Essays on the Novel by Henry James, ed. L. Edel (London: Rupert Hart-Davis, 1957).
Literary Reviews and Essays by Henry James, ed. A. Mordell (New York: Twayne, 1957).
James, Henry, *French Writers and American Women*, ed. P. Buitenhius (Branford, Conn.: Compass, 1960).
Henry James: Selected Literary Criticism, ed. M. Shapira (London: Heinemann, 1963).
James, Henry, *Literary Criticism*, 2 vols (New York: Literary Classics of the United States, 1984).

(iv) Letters, Notebooks

Hasler, J., *Switzerland in the Life and Work of Henry James: The Clare Benedict Collection of Letters from Henry James* (Bern: Francke, 1966).
James, Henry, *The Complete Notebooks*, ed. L. Edel and L. H. Powers (New York: Oxford University Press, 1987).
James, Henry, *Henry James Letters*, ed. L. Edel (vols I–III, London: Macmillan, 1975, 1978 and 1980; vol. IV, Cambridge, Mass. and London: Belknap Press of Harvard University Press, 1984).
James, Henry, *The Letters of Henry James*, ed. P. Lubbock (London: Macmillan, 1920).
James, Henry, *The Notebooks of Henry James*, ed. F. O. Matthiessen and K. B. Murdock (New York: Oxford University Press, 1947).

James, Henry, *Selected Letters of Henry James*, ed. L. Edel (London: Rupert Hart-Davis, 1955).
James, Henry, and Wells, H. G., *Henry James and H. G. Wells: A Record*, ed. L. Edel and G. N. Ray (London: Rupert Hart-Davis, 1958).

AUTOBIOGRAPHY AND BIOGRAPHY

Edel, L., *Henry James* (London: Rupert Hart-Davis; *The Untried Years*, 1953; *The Conquest of London*, 1962; *The Middle Years*, 1963; *The Treacherous Years*, 1969; *The Master*, 1972).
Hyde, H. Montgomery, *Henry James at Home* (London: Methuen, 1969).
James, Henry, *A Small Boy and Others* (London: Macmillan, 1913).
James, Henry, *Notes of a Son and Brother* (London: Macmillan, 1914).
James, Henry, *The Middle Years* (London: Collins, 1917).
Matthiessen, F. O., *The James Family* (New York: Knopf, 1947).
Nowell-Smith, F., *The Legend of the Master* (London: Constable, 1947).
Page, N., *Henry James: Interviews and Recollections* (London: Macmillan, 1984).

BIBLIOGRAPHY

Blanck, J., 'Henry James', in *Bibliography of American Literature*, 5 vols (New Haven, Conn.: Yale University Press, 1955–69), vol. V, pp. 117–81.
Budd, J., *A Bibliography of Criticism, 1975–1981* (Westpoint, Conn.: Greenwood, 1983).
Edel, L. and Laurence, D. H., *A Bibliography of Henry James*, 3rd ed., revised by James Rambeau (Clarendon Press: Oxford, 1982).
McColgan, K. P., *Henry James, 1917–1959: A Reference Guide* (Boston, Mass.: Hall, 1979).
Phillips, Le Roy, *A Bibliography of the Writings of Henry James* (Boston, Mass.: Houghton Mifflin, 1906).
Ricks, B., *Henry James: A Bibliography of Secondary Works* (Metuchen, N.J.: Scarecrow, 1975).
Scura, D. M., *Henry James, 1960–1974: A Reference Guide* (Boston, Mass.: Hall, 1979).

SELECTED CRITICISM

Anderson, C. R., *Person, Place and Thing in Henry James's Novels* (Durham, N.C.: Duke University Press, 1977).
Anderson, Q., *The American Henry James* (New Brunswick, N.J.: Rutgers University Press, 1957).
Bell, Ian F. A. (ed.), *Henry James: Fiction as History* (London and Totowa, N.J.: Vision and Barnes and Noble, 1984 and 1985).

Bellringer, A. W., *The Ambassadors* (London: Allen and Unwin, 1984).

Berland, A., *Culture and Conduct in the Novels of Henry James* (Cambridge: Cambridge University Press, 1981).

Bewley, M., *The Complex Fate* (London: Chatto and Windus, 1952).

Bradbury, N., *Henry James: The Later Novels* (Oxford: Clarendon Press, 1979).

Buitenhuis, N., *The Grasping Imagination: The American Writings of Henry James* (Toronto: University of Toronto Press, 1970).

Cargill, O., *The Novels of Henry James* (New York: Macmillan, 1961).

Donadio, S., *Nietzsche, Henry James, and the Artistic Will* (London: Oxford University Press, 1978).

Dupee, F. W., *Henry James* (New York: Sloane, 1951).

Dupee, F. W. (ed.), *The Question of Henry James: A Collection of Critical Essays* (London: Allen Wingate, 1945).

Eakin, P. J., *The New England Girl* (Athens, Ga.: University of Georgia Press, 1976).

Edel, L. (ed.), *Henry James: A Collection of Critical Essays* (Englewood Cliffs, N.J.: Prentice-Hall, 1963).

Fowler, V. C., *Henry James's American Girl* (Madison, Wis.: University of Wisconsin Press, 1984).

Gale, R. L., *The Caught Image: Figurative Language in the Fiction of Henry James* (Chapel Hill, N.C.: University of North Carolina Press, 1964).

Gard, R., *Henry James: The Critical Heritage* (London: Routledge and Kegan Paul, 1968).

Geismar, M., *Henry James and the Jacobites* (Boston, Mass.: Houghton Mifflin, 1963), also published as *Henry James and his Cult* (London: Chatto and Windus, 1964).

Goode, J. (ed.), *The Air of Reality: New Essays on Henry James* (London: Methuen, 1972).

Graham, K., *Henry James: The Drama of Fulfilment* (Oxford: Clarendon Press, 1975).

Holland, L. B., *The Experience of Vision: Essays on the Craft of Henry James* (Princeton: Princeton University Press, 1964).

Hutchinson, S., *Henry James: An American as Modernist* (London and Totowa, N.J.: Vision and Barnes and Noble, 1982 and 1983).

Isle, W., *Experiments in Form: Henry James's Novels: 1896–1901* (London: Oxford University Press, 1968).

Jefferson, D. W., *Henry James and the Modern Reader* (Edinburgh and London: Oliver and Boyd, 1964).

Kappeler, S., *Writing and Reading in Henry James* (London: Macmillan, 1980).

Kelley, C. P., *The Early Development of Henry James* (Urbana, Ill.: University of Illinois Press, 1930).

Krook, D., *The Ordeal of Consciousness in Henry James* (Cambridge: Cambridge University Press, 1962).

Leavis, F. R., *The Common Pursuit* (London: Chatto and Windus, 1952).

Leavis, F. R., *The Great Tradition* (London: Chatto and Windus, 1948).

Lebowitz, N., *The Imagination of Loving: Henry James's Legacy to the Novel* (Detroit: Wayne State University Press, 1965).

Lee, B., *The Novels of Henry James: A Study of Culture and Consciousness* (London: Arnold, 1978).

Mull, D. L., *Henry James's 'Sublime Economy': Money as Symbolic Center in the Fiction* (Middletown, Conn.: Wesleyan University Press, 1973).

Perosa, S., *Henry James and the Experimental Novel* (Charlottesville, Va.: University of Virginia Press, 1978).

Poirier, R., *The Comic Sense of Henry James* (London: Chatto and Windus, 1960).

Purdy, S. B., *The Hole in the Fabric: Silence, Contemporary Literature and Henry James* (Pittsburgh: Pittsburgh University Press, 1977).

Putt, S. G., *A Reader's Guide to Henry James* (London: Thames and Hudson, 1966).

Sears, S., *The Negative and Imagination: Form and Perspective in the Novels of Henry James* (Ithaca, N.Y.: Cornell University Press, 1968).

Segal, O., *The Lucid Reflector: The Observer in Henry James's Fiction* (New Haven, Conn.: Yale University Press, 1969).

Seltzer, M., *Henry James and the Art of Power* (Ithaca, N.Y.: Cornell University Press, 1984).

Sharp, M. C., *The Confidante in Henry James* (Notre Dame, Ind.: Indiana University Press, 1963).

Stewart, J. I. M., *Eight Modern Writers* (Oxford: Clarendon Press, 1963).

Tanner, T. (ed.), *Henry James: Modern Judgments* (London: Macmillan, 1968).

Veeder, W. R., *Henry James: The Lessons of the Master* (Chicago: University of Chicago Press, 1975).

Wagenknecht, E., *The Novels of Henry James* (New York: Ungar, 1983).

Wagenknecht, E., *The Tales of Henry James* (New York: Ungar, 1984).

Ward, J. A., *The Imagination of Disaster: Evil in the Fiction of Henry James* (Lincoln, Na.: University of Nebraska Press, 1961).

Wegelin, C., *The Image of Europe in Henry James* (Dallas: Southern Methodist University Press, 1958).

Yeazell, R. B., *Language and Knowledge in the Late Novels of Henry James* (Chicago: University of Chicago Press, 1976).

Index

150